O that God would grant that my commentaries and those of all other teachers were destroyed, and that every Christian took the Bible in his own hands, and read God's word for himself. You would then see that there is an infinite difference between the word of God and the word of man; and that no man, with all he may himself say, can do more than understand and explain properly a part of God's word. So dig deeper, ever deeper, my brethren. Let my explanations and those of others serve merely as scaffolding to the real building, in order that we may grasp the pure and sweet word of God, and feed on it, and stand by it: for God alone dwells in Zion.

Martin Luther

HOW TO READ

THE
BIBLE

A. J. CONYERS

INTERVARSITY PRESS
DOWNERS GROVE, ILLINOIS 60515

1986

InterVarsity Press is the book-publishing division of Inter-Varsity Christian Fellowship, a student movement active on campus at hundreds of universities, colleges and schools of nursing. For information about local and regional activities, write IVCF, 233 Langdon St., Madison, WI 53703.

The Scripture quotations contained herein, unless otherwise noted, are from the Revised Standard Version of the Bible copyrighted 1946, 1952, 1971 by the Division of Christian Education of the National Council of the Churches of Christ in the U.S.A. and are used by permission. All rights reserved.

Distributed in Canada through InterVarsity Press, 860 Denison St., Unit 3, Markham, Ontario L3R 4H1, Canada.

Cover illustration: Roberta Polfus

ISBN 0-87784-944-7
ISBN 0-87784-946-3 (How to Read series)

Printed in the United States of America

Library of Congress Cataloguing in Publication Data
Conyers, A. J., 1944-
   How to read the Bible.

   Bibliography: p.
   1. Bible—Reading.   2. Bible—Study.   I. Title.
BS167.C64   1986   220'.07   85-23173
ISBN 0-87784-944-7

| 18 | 17 | 16 | 15 | 14 | 13 | 12 | 11 | 10 | 9 | 8 | 7 | 6 | 5 | 4 | 3 | 2 | 1 |
| 99 | 98 | 97 | 96 | 95 | 94 | 93 | 92 | 91 | 90 | 89 | 88 | 87 | 86 | | | | |

THE HOW TO READ SERIES

The Bible is one book, yet it consists of many—history and wisdom, prophecy and apocalyptic, poetry and letters, law and narrative. This variety, while it enriches us, also challenges us. How are we to comprehend the unique contribution each type of literature makes to our understanding of God and our world?

The How to Read series is designed for nonprofessionals who want a professional understanding of Scripture. Each volume is written by an expert and focuses on one type of biblical literature, explaining its unique features and how these features should shape the way we approach it. The goal throughout is to help us all better understand the Bible and apply it to our lives.

To Deborah

Introduction:
An Invitation
to Bible
Reading

An underlying conviction has carried forward the writing of every chapter in this book. It is simply that the Christian community needs to recapture the vocabulary and grammar of faith. We need the power to express the things we believe and experience: the ability to tell the story, to explain and defend the doctrines, to pray and to proclaim the wonder of Christ's presence in the world.

If my informal observations can be trusted and there is in fact a dearth of this ability to express the faith, then the fault lies at every level, among clergy as well as laity. Adults are often unable to guide children. Experienced Christians feel they can't teach new converts. Many are timid about confessing Christ to unbelievers: their heart fails them, in part, because words have failed them.

I am convinced, however, that the remedy lies close at hand. Down through the centuries the Bible has given us the means for speaking about our faith and the God of our faith. These are the words of life. No other vocabulary has been found adequate to the task. Insight into our growth toward maturity is strengthened by exposure to mature concepts, and we find these in the apostles and prophets. The ties that bind the church and the Christian family together are woven from biblical words of love and commitment. The authority that sends the church outward into the world is transmitted to us through the Bible, so that both the message and the mandate of the church depend on the language of Scripture. To recover the grammar and vocabulary of faith—that language by which its invisible power is clothed and becomes known to us—is to reacquaint ourselves with the Bible.

I do not mean that people ought to speak a "Bible language" with constant references to Scripture texts. Quite to the contrary. Our everyday thinking, feeling and speaking is an unconscious product of the life of the mind and the experiences of the soul. If our imaginations have been engaged by the accounts of great saints and prophets, if our thoughts are fashioned by themes from Paul, if our hearts have learned to recognize the psalmist's thirst for the everlasting God, then we have been given an expanded frame of reference, a grammar for understanding life—and for expressing the Christian faith. David's experience has been partially absorbed into our own, through the agency of his songs. Paul's conviction has been given access to our minds, through his words. Christ's own call to discipleship transcends the centuries, and we each hear the voice that says "Come, take up your cross, and follow me." And all of this becomes a living experience because of the work of the Holy Spirit.

The Practical Task

The concepts and the methods I outline here emphasize ways of actually reading the Bible. It seems to me that academic training has erred in one direction at the introductory level of Bible study, and popular methods have often erred in precisely the opposite direction. Too frequently college students are encouraged to study the Bible by reading *about* the Bible. No matter how good their textbooks might be, students are done a disservice if their textbooks absorb more attention than the Bible itself. It is a little like enrolling in a class on Shakespeare, reading several works of learned criticism, and never reading *Hamlet*.

On the other hand, popular Bible study methods often feature ingenious ways of studying the text—its words, its principle characters, its personal application and so forth—without ever reading Scripture to gain its original intention or content.

Beginning in chapter four, I suggest an approach to Bible study that encourages reading the books themselves. Other reading is strictly secondary. Methods of straining the texts through various systems of examination are also secondary—although they are many times helpful. There is sufficient reason, which I hope to make clear, that the Bible needs to be viewed in much the same way as it was seen by its earliest readers; that is, in terms of individual books. The first readers did not have in hand verses or chapters; they had letters and gospels and prophecies. Our present habit of going directly to a small segment of a book and confining ourselves to that can only be profitable against the background of knowing the book as it was originally intended to be read.

One needs also to be able to read Scripture sometimes without even the thought of mining it for personal lessons or practical recommendations—these will come, but the best ones take us by surprise. The classic attraction of the Bible, that which gives it pre-eminence above all other books, is that its message is true and that it therefore gives meaning to life. To say that the Bible is practical and gives a method for living is a statement that can certainly be defended, but it is not the highest estimation of the Bible's worth. These words are to us life and joy because they give us a view of the world, of man and of God that is true and foundational for all else.

A Small Caveat

In a course on art appreciation back in my college days, we were instructed on how to "see" a painting. Here is the point of light the eye would catch first, we were told, and then the eye would follow certain lines until it surveyed the entire canvas. Here was a subtle gesture, or a sudden dramatic movement, that evokes in us a precise response—revulsion, attraction, fore-boding, hope. Thus we were trained to "see" what we might have expected to speak for itself.

Isn't there at least a hint of presumption in teaching this way? Surely the task is necessary, but can't the question be raised anyway, and can't the reserve and modesty with which we approach such instruction be a valuable companion to the task? After all, each viewer views a painting in his own way. And our reservations about art appreciation arise from a confidence that good painters can speak through their painting without the help of an art instructor.

The same kind of question at least bears a moment's thought when the subject is how to read the Bible. In a way that is true of every book but intensely true of this one; we each read the Bible in our own way. We come at this book with vastly different experiences, motives, levels of interest, and with quite individual expectations.

It is not, after all, technical expertise that Scripture itself urges upon the reader, but humility to accept the teaching authority of the Holy Word that is provided and illuminated by the Holy Spirit. Expertise enforces standards and encourages conformity; reliance on the Spirit threatens conformity. One relies on the community of scholars, the other on the unrepeatable moment in one person's life.

Individuality and the unique mark the highest moments in Bible reading for other reasons. For one, our irreducible personality, distinct from every other soul on earth, unique in relation to the entire span of history, is drawn into a circle of companions. We each come to know the soul's hunger of David, the anguish of Jeremiah, the burning conviction of Paul. The response to such an encounter is unpredictable. It is not, nor should it be, governed by rules and techniques.

Such a reading of the Bible, then, does not invite heavy-handed suggestions that impose on the uniqueness of this encounter. To impose an approach upon Bible readers may presume upon the freedom essential to the very heart of our purpose in reading the Bible. Just so, art does not welcome interpretation, and no matter how excellent the interpretive powers, they cannot escape having the air of artificiality: the artwork itself is intended to communicate and not to be communicated through another medium. Such cannot be any less true of the Bible.

The Need to Know How to Read

There is another side to this question or else there would be no purpose for this book.

At the Art Institute of Chicago not long ago, I stood before a painting that held my attention like no other painting I saw that day. It left its mark on me for days. It was the most powerful image I had ever witnessed concerning the burial of Christ.

The effect of this painting struck me as being quite spontaneous. But there were rather precise features of the painting that I noticed, and that helped to form my impression.

The painting recalled the entombment of Christ. I quickly noticed that almost all the eyes in the painting were focused on the pale, dead body of Jesus. Gentleness was the prevailing tone and attitude. One figure, however, stood only slightly to the side. Her tear-stained face was turned away from the bitter task of lowering the corpse into the sepulchre. Her eyes were cast upward toward heaven, as if to ask the question, "Where is God?" Her one slight gesture anticipated, amid this almost unrelieved gloom, the resurrection of Christ.

But how did these thoughts of mine occur when I witnessed the painting? I was observing this painting with the help of concepts I had learned from someone who instructs in how to "see" a painting. Was my reaction, then, less spontaneous than if my observations had been innocent of any training?

I think the answer must be no. There *is* a difference, however. And the difference is this: After learning how others viewed a painting, the possibilities within the experience were expanded for me; spontaneity is not quenched, but it is actually enhanced and stimulated by the presence of training. Freedom is not spoiled when one learns the skills for living in adult society—how to drive, how to write a check, how to read and

write—but it is all the more established, because the possibilities are increased.

You can read the Bible, of course, if you can read at all. But
to read the Bible and know the full range of its message is
another kind of experience. And it is worthy of our careful
preparation and best efforts.

PART I
The Art of Bible Reading

The Bible is both a divine and human book. First and foremost it records God's self-disclosure and his saving purpose in Christ. Yet God reveals himself primarily in and through the events of history, through the experiences of those he calls to himself. Therefore the Bible must be seen in light of two important principles: (1) it is a book of history, and (2) it is a book of faith. These two principles are the chief pillars in the edifice of Bible study. Without one or the other we lose a proper perspective; taken together, they are the most comprehensive supports for Scripture interpretation.

1
A Preface
to Bible
Reading

The first rule for reading, said Mortimer Adler in *How to Read a Book,* is this: "You must know what kind of book you are reading, and you should know this as early in the process as possible, preferably before you begin to read."[1]

People frequently read the Bible, of course, without knowing precisely what kind of book it is, and without even suspecting what theologians and biblical scholars say about it. It may not impress them greatly, for instance, that the Bible is a collection of several types of writing. Nevertheless, as a general rule they profit from their reading anyway. The Bible is *that* kind of book: it doesn't always have to wait for explanations.

I don't want to dismiss Adler's first rule for reading quite that easily, however. We have good reason to believe that it can be put to good use in reading the Bible as well as any other book—perhaps even better use. That is why, in this section, I want to set forth some basic thoughts about what kind of book we are reading when we read the Bible.

One Encounter with the Bible
Kunsiri, a young government official from Bangkok engaged in

graduate study at the university where I teach, arrived at my office, pulled a small tape recorder from her purse and placed it on my desk. "Do you mind?" she asked.

"No," I said. We had been through this before. Kunsiri was inching her way to Christianity along an intellectual labyrinth.

"Why do Christians believe that Jesus Christ is the Son of God? Why are there so many denominations in Christianity? I like what you say about love, but how do Christians know that God loves them?" The questions were basic and thoughtful. She pursued issues with relentless rigor, beginning with a deceptively simple question and then quickly seeing the complex side.

She attended church. At first, there was only a detached curiosity. And then more: she heard the gospel preached and taught; she read the Bible in English and in Thai. All the time it was one of the loneliest periods of her life. What she found in the Christian message and in the example of Christians— a certain quality of love—had a solid appeal to her. It was something, she said, that was not found so distinctly in her own faith. And now she was in a circumstance, as a stranger in a strange land, to know how much she needed it.

Soon she met Youyen, another Thai graduate student who had only recently become a Christian. Youyen wanted to lead Kunsiri to Christ. But the doubts, the multiplying questions, the loyalty to old ways, and a dread of responding to Christianity only out of a desperate loneliness, formed barriers to Kunsiri's receiving the gospel with faith.

Then one day she told me she had concluded her search. "I've decided I want to be baptized," she said. She spoke in the precise, even tones I had become accustomed to hearing.

I suppose I registered some surprise at first, not expecting, after months of pondering, to see her come so suddenly to a decision. I asked her about it.

"Yesterday," she said, "after church, I was studying at my desk. I began to think about Youyen, and how she was when I saw her in church. I left my book on the desk, walked over to the window and looked out. Suddenly, it came to me that Someone really loved me, and *always had.*"

This testimony of the keenly rational graduate student was not one of a rational discovery. It was a leap in understanding—a titanic shift in her world that caused her to see it from an entirely new angle. How suddenly she realized something she had always known. "Someone loves me," she now realized. But just as suddenly, she realized that "He *always had.*"

Although it may not be immediately apparent, I think this experience shows something important about the way the Bible operates on lives that are exposed to its message. That message may be preached, taught or read, but it is the Bible, and we would hardly know the message without the Bible.

How did Kunsiri come to Christ? By discovering something she had, in some sense, at some level, always known. Why did she make the discovery? Because the gospel—preached, taught and read—had given her a language by which she could understand the experience. The experienced need for the love of God had, in some way, been there before, but it required a word from the outside to bring it to the surface and create out of it a new and all-encompassing vision of life. The Bible, in the various ways it came to her, had done that.

What Kind of Book?
How can we ascribe to the Bible such a telling effect? What is it that sets off the Bible from other writings in this regard?

In the first place, behind the Bible lies a fundamental conviction. It is that God communicates himself to us. The word of God is borne along by creation itself according to Romans 1 and Psalm 19. And it comes to sharper focus in history, especially in the history of Israel, and supremely in Israel's Messiah.

But why a written word? How is it that these all-encompassing media—creation and history—are thrust into the background while Scripture alone becomes the oracle of faith?

With regard to creation, the answer in Scripture itself is clear. Because of sin, the word in creation has become ambiguous. It hints at what our hearts know must be there, but our eyes have not seen clearly. The word in history recedes from us, and the memory of it slips like sand from our grasp. There must be

a continuing word. It must be a witness to those innocent of
bondage in Egypt, who never saw a cross except as a gilded
ornament between two candles, and who stand too far from the
resurrection to catch its brilliance or to be stunned by the announcement that the crucified one has been raised from the
dead. There must be an aid to our memories and a light that
kindles and recreates within us experiences and hopes that
once pressed on men and women from every side. There must
be a faithful reminder that God still speaks, and acts, and waits,
and loves—one that reminds us how to recognize God's word
in the world around us and in the history of our lives. This, too,
is the word of God. "You will do well to pay attention to this
[word] as to a lamp shining in a dark place, until the day dawns
and the morning star rises in your hearts" (2 Pet 1:19).

The Inspired Word
But why this word and no other? The question is not resolved
easily. A point of departure, however, are the three fundamental and irreducible claims that Scripture makes for itself: it is
inspired, it is authoritative, and it is a living word.

First, Scripture says of itself that it is inspired. When we read
that "all scripture is inspired by God and profitable for teaching, for reproof, for correction, and for training in righteousness" (2 Tim 3:16), Paul is obviously referring, at that early date,
to the Old Testament. The New Testament, of course, was still
in its formative stage while the Old Testament, and for the most
part the Greek translation of the Hebrew text, was the Scripture
of first-century Christians. But when Peter refers to the letters
of Paul, he calls them Scripture (2 Pet 3:15-16). Even before the
New Testament was drawn together and considered authoritative canon, parts of it were being drawn into the circle of writings recognized as inspired. So we might justifiably say that this
term *inspired* takes in all of what we commonly call Scripture.

Evidently the New Testament writers are suggesting that
there is something different, something peculiar, about these
writings—all of these that are called Scripture, the whole of
which, according to 2 Timothy, are to be considered inspired

by God. But what precisely is the difference implied here? The word that is translated "inspired by God" is found only once in the Bible (2 Tim 3:16); however, the idea it conveys is broadly and almost continuously implied. The word is *theopneustos,* "God-breathed." Scripture comes because of the operation of the Spirit of God; it is breathed full of the life-giving power and truth of God. One can find a faithful guide here, because it is, after all, God who caused these things to be remembered and written down and interpreted. However much of it is human history in the books of Samuel and Kings, the recalling of it shows how God looked and felt to a growing nation. However much of the Psalms are human praise, they are lifted up and made worthy of their heavenly Object because it was God who acted to draw forth such praise. However much of Ecclesiastes is a journal of human doubt, it gives us a clear picture of life without God, thus setting in relief the dimensions of a God-filled life. And in every case the word is ultimately seen not as a human word in an autonomous and unaided sense, but rather as a God-inspired word.

But the idea of inspiration must not be confused with the notion that God dictated words to automatons who then wrote, not their own thoughts, but those of a mind utterly alien to their own. It is true that in parts of Scripture, notably in writings like Judges that reflect on the earliest national life of Israel, we find men and women moved about and used in a way that implies they had little if anything to do with the matter. Gideon was "possessed" by the Spirit of God; God clothed himself in Gideon and used him to strike the enemy. The Spirit of God came upon Samson, and he performed deeds of a magnitude that would never be expected of a normal man, or even of a very strong and skillful man.

Nevertheless, this is far from the later view, and the more typical view, of how God led in the writing of Scripture. The word "inspired"—*theopneustos*—is a much gentler and subtler word than "possession." The ego, the personality of the writer, is not thrust into the background; instead it is, if anything, brought more clearly into focus, heightened and energized as

the Spirit moves it to write. It is no small consequence that
Amos wrote one prophecy and Hosea another. Their personalities are intact, and they become a part of the message itself.
The message of Jeremiah is given its peculiar force and its
expressive pathos because it was written by a very real and very
human Jeremiah.

In fact, we might say that the essential meaning of inspiration
is that, by it, God communicates not simply a message but the
messenger—a whole personality. By moving the biblical authors to write as he did, we are given a view not only of what
they thought, but also of what they felt, how they doubted, and
what caused them to grow. Not only does he bring to bear on
us as readers certain thoughtful ideas, but he confronts us with
the messenger himself, including his experience, his hopes and
his fears. In reading Amos we are not simply reading ideas
about God, rather we are confronted with a very real prophet
named Amos who had an encounter with God.

Thus if we read attentively and sympathetically, we are drawn
into the midst of an experience—an experience that involved
not only the mind, but the heart as well. Our hearts respond
to an experience of long ago, and a new flame is kindled over
the chasm of two millennia. Once again we stand in the presence of the living God by the agency of words that transmit that
experience from the time it burned its way into the lives of
prophets and saints.

The Authoritative Word

The authority of these writings is related to the idea of their
inspiration. But the question of authority comes up when you
ask, "Why are these writings included and others excluded?"
Are these books, in fact, the *only* way God speaks to us?

Karl Barth, for one, warns against an authority that is divided
between the Bible and something else. Klaas Runia aptly expressed the Barthian position: "Once on the road of a theology
which says, 'and' (Scripture *and* Tradition), the 'ands' appear
everywhere: Faith *and* works, nature *and* grace, reason *and* revelation."[2]

However, for most of Christian history, that exclusive either/ or position has not been maintained. For Augustine the authority of Scripture was based on the authority of the church. Among the Protestant Reformers the emphasis was certainly on the supreme authority of Scripture, but even Luther did not ascribe equal authority to all Scripture. The New Testament, for him, had greater authority than the Old; and the books of Hebrews, James and Revelation were of questionable value. Zwingli even considered some of the insights of Plato and Seneca to be the work of the Holy Spirit. Evidently these, all of whom affirmed the authority of Scripture, had in mind a specific *kind* of authority.

For the meaning of scriptural authority we have to look closer at the purpose of Scripture, the reasons for its selection over other works considered to be helpful or truthful by the early church. I think we have a clue in the word the church used in selecting an exclusive list of writings as Scripture.

The word is *canon*. The original meaning of *canon*, borrowed from a word referring to a reed, was that of a measuring rod, a standard of measure. Scripture was considered canon because it could be used as a standard to measure the truth of other writings, other statements, other witnesses. It does not exclusively tell the truth, but it tells the truth exclusively. Others may have valid insights, true experiences, genuine motives—but here are the products of apostles and prophets who can be trusted, because the Holy Spirit has given witness that their word is God-breathed. They are not the only ones who speak truth or who have had genuine knowledge of God, but against this standard all else can be measured and its value tested. A yardstick may not be the only thing in the world that is a yard long, but at least a seamstress can be assured that a yardstick is a yard long and that other things can be measured by it.

In this way of thinking about Scripture, the "both/and" is no threat to the authority of Scripture. In fact as the truth of Scripture is confirmed by experience (tradition is no more nor less than collective experience), or by reason (science is only a limited and disciplined use of reason), or by new moral insights (the conviction that slavery is wrong is no less than an extension of the Christian teachings on the love of God for *all* people), the authority of Scripture is not diluted, but established all the more. By the same token, the problem with the either/or thinking of some is that the exclusive truth of Scripture, or of special revelation, drives the truth of God out of the world and gives revealed truth no place to lodge. Not only is it not of the world, it is against the world and falsifies everything else. There is no one to respond to that truth; no one who even recognizes it.

The early gnostics were the masters of this style of thought. And the effect of their thinking was to drive a wedge into the world, splitting apart good and evil, truth and falsehood, splitting apart the world of nature and the world of humanity.

Authentic Christian thinking does just the opposite. Evil is given no positive existence; rather, all things are created good, and the world along with humanity is the object of redemption to a loving God. Nothing escapes his loving attention (not even the sparrow); nothing escapes the truth and beauty (not even the lily of the field) which God spreads abroad. Malcolm Muggeridge expressed it well when he said that the world speaks of God, but its message is written in code which keeps us from understanding clearly what it says, and the Bible is the code book. When the world is seen through the eyes of one who has absorbed the biblical message, its truth and its beauty speak with abundant clarity.

The Living Word

Many debates surround what is called the inner witness of the Holy Spirit, an interior witness that testifies to the truth of the exterior word, that is, to the truth of Scripture. Some stress the church as the custodian of that truth and as the authoritative guide to interpreting Scripture. Others see that witness as immediate and individual, and without reference to the corporate experience of the church. The former emphasis is typical of the Roman Catholic Church; the latter is typical of "enthusiasm" in its many historical forms.

Between these two extremes is a broad area that takes on many different expressions. But the important thing to note—and it is so important and so pervasive that it can often be missed simply because it is common and likely to be taken for granted—the principal matter that pervades this whole discussion is that Scripture is not a dead letter, but a living witness.

To read Scripture is to awaken a consciousness of God. To encounter God in the witness of the prophets or the apostles is to stimulate a desire and a thirst within one's own heart for the Word of God. The inner word is an operation of the Holy Spirit; so was the outer written word a result of the Spirit's work. One witness calls forth the other, just as music awakens the desire of music and the laughter of children recalls the joys of innocence. The company of a genuinely good person may not remind you of your own goodness, but it makes you aware of certain qualities, even of how much those qualities are missed. Those figures of the Old and New Testaments who have had their lives filled to the full may incidently remind us of how empty we are, but they also make us aware of a living desire for God. The Holy Spirit works both to convict us of our emptiness and to invite us to the feast. He provides the word from ancient times, and he spans the ages between to make the word a living reality within those who read, hear and believe.

Therefore, the writer of Hebrews could say, "The word of God is living and active, sharper than any two-edged sword, piercing to the division of soul and spirit, of joints and marrow, and discerning the thoughts and intentions of the heart" (Heb 4:12). This is the principal thing that serious students of the Bible must discover. With willing hearts and open minds they will confirm what men and women have said about Scripture from ancient times. Only now their words become living reality.

2
How to
Read Bible
History

When we read the Bible we are reading a book about God, "with whom there is no variation or shadow due to change" (Jas 1:17). And yet, what this book gives us, more than anything else, is the variableness, the changes and the particularity of history.

A question naturally arises. How can the Bible outline the pertinent features of the creator God "who made the Pleiades and Orion" by telling us about a man and his disciples on their dusty pilgrimage through remote villages on the eastern edge of the Mediterranean Sea?

A bright Kenyan student of mine raised the question while we were reading Genesis. Thoughts began to plague him about why God would use Jacob for his purposes, as the patriarchal head of his covenant people. Couldn't God have done better? Surely there were finer characters, with at least the most common virtues of loyalty and affection toward the family. Even Esau possessed some qualities that recommended him more than Jacob. Why would God have chosen *this* man with his all-too-obvious flaws?

The problem is that we want to talk in universals and this book gives us particulars. When we ask for abstracts about an invisible God, it gives us concretes about visible people. All we want to know about is that which is holy, righteous and beyond question; instead it tells us about Jacob—lying, cheating, equivocal Jacob. Our questions about abstract ideals are constantly answered with the concreteness of history. How could that possibly tell us about God?

An extraordinary story about Moses in the book of Exodus helps us understand this distinctive Hebrew (and later, Christian) way of speaking about God. The story is one of those perfectly cut gems, set deep within Scripture, that somehow reflects light on all the rest.

Moses and the Search for Understanding

In a brief episode Moses makes two requests that, in effect, put brackets around everything the Bible says about God's disclosure of himself to us. First Moses asks, "If I have found favor in thy sight, show me now thy ways, that I may know thee and find favor in thy sight" (Ex 33:13). Notice the specific request to know "thy ways," to know God by his actions. Or, in other words, by the events he brings to pass. God answers positively: "This very thing that you have spoken I will do; for you have found favor in my sight, and I know you by name" (v. 17). God will reveal himself by the history of his actions among his people. It is through events that they will understand and know him, and it is because of a personal relationship ("I know you by name") that their reading of history becomes an understanding of God.

I can remember when the idea of giving testimonies in church was not looked on with favor by people in the "better" churches. Happily that kind of restraint is disappearing and many churches are returning to what is a quite natural practice for Christians. Giving an account of our experience of God— whether that be the story of our conversion, how we discovered God's will, how we received aid and comfort in a time of trial, or whatever—reflects perfectly the Christian understanding of faith. People know God by what he has *done* in their lives. The story of God is the story of what actually happened to them. It may have been miraculous, or it may seem quite ordinary to the outside observer. In either case they have perceived God's hand in the events of their lives.

Therefore, a testimony relates an indirect (not at all a direct) experience of God. It is important in fact to note that what Christians know of God comes indirectly. We could claim, of course, to have seen God and try to describe him, giving an account of our conversation with God, but we better be ready for some incredulous looks on the faces of our hearers. In that sense almost all churches would be rather staid in their attitudes.

But why are churches so reluctant at that point? Why, in the normal expression of the Christian faith, do we always find this decided preference for an indirect, historical knowledge of God?

Strong tradition, of course, undergirds this way of thinking. We take it very much for granted. And we can do so because our world, to an extent that is often not acknowledged, has been more or less thoroughly convinced of the biblical view of reality. It is a view that naturally has us talking about God as someone who leaves traces of himself in human experience—footprints, as it were, in history.

If we tried to determine why this way of thinking about God came to be so natural for the Jewish and Christian expression of faith, or why the world at large found it so convincing, I think we are led to three basic ideas.

The first is simply that the Bible itself shows an enormous interest in history. Who is God? He is the God of Abraham, Isaac and Jacob. He is the God who led Israel out of bondage in Egypt. From creation to the Incarnation, the biblical witness draws its language about God from the memory and the expectations of history.

At the same time, the Bible shows a decided lack of interest in describing reality that cannot be observed in history. The Bible says very little about heaven and hell—quite a lot less than we need to satisfy our curiosity. The pictures we get of angels and demons are mere suggestions—they are never very clear. We are left only to wonder at the veiled mysteries of other worlds. In this very reluctance to deal directly and expansively, we see a vivid contrast to the mythologies of the Greeks, Romans, Babylonians and others. But more importantly, this virtual absence of the mythologies so common to the ancient world underscores the Bible's obvious preference to focus on only one level of reality—that which we experience as history.

A second consideration is that the result of this focus on history is to suggest that there is *more* than what we observe. It suggests that something lies beyond and behind history. Furthermore, while mythical stories of the gods and their affairs tend to describe those gods, they furnish the imagination with a positive image of the divine powers. The focus on history, in contrast, does something entirely different to our imagination. The God whose effects are known in history is only hinted at; the parting of the sea, the plagues that afflicted Egypt only *begin* to tell us about this God. Who knows what power and what mystery lurk behind these events? A powerful suggestion is created out of the events of history: the reality that lies behind those works may well be boundless.

One further matter to consider is that a direct vision, or a mythical description of God, strongly suggests that we can somehow "take God in." It suggests that since he can be described he can also be *circumscribed,* and the mode of his existence known. It suggests that he can be domesticated and brought down to our own level. But what of the God who can only be known by the trace of his hand in the affairs of men and nations? A German proverb says, "A comprehended God is no God." Such a conviction of the enormity of a God who lies far beyond our mental grasp is exactly the point. It is precisely the effect of the biblical route to the disclosure of God in history: he cannot be imagined—therefore, "Thou shalt make no images."

Moses' first request, then, opens the way to understanding how God reveals himself in biblical history. The other request, however, closes the brackets; it shows how Scripture definitely does *not* claim to know God. Moses' one other request went vastly farther than his first one: "I pray thee, show me thy glory."

That is, "Show me visibly and finally an image of thyself." All could be experienced in a final epiphany. Moses didn't have the patience to wait for a Hegel to give him that epiphany: God as a dialectical formula. Or for a Marx: an ideological touchstone as a replacement for God or Spirit. Modern ideologies would hope to sum up reality in a single paragraph, a single vision. That is what Moses hoped for—God's nature, God's will, God's glory, all concentrated in a moment of being. The request is similar to Philip's when he asks Jesus, "Show us the Father and it will satisfy us."

Moses perhaps couldn't have realized yet that what God wished to reveal could not be shown in a sudden epiphany. No single experience can exhaust what is to be known about God, and even a lifetime of experience can be, at best, only partial and incomplete. For God to fully disclose himself to us would require one of two things. Either God would represent himself in a manner that is altogether inadequate in one vision, at one time, in a certain way, to one person—he would *misrepresent* himself, in other words—*or* he would burst the frame of human life and understanding.

Such is a dangerous prospect, he assured Moses: "You cannot see my face; for man shall not see me and live." Finite man runs great risks when he opens himself to the infinite! When he loses his finitude, he loses himself. Shapes, sounds, bodies— all of finite things—exist by virtue of their limits. A sound is a sound because of pitch and tone; to conceive of infinite sound is to conceive of no sound at all. Bodies of all sorts have shape and bulk and are what they are because of a certain definition, because of limits. Infinity threatens finitude; eternity threatens the temporal. The presence of God always calls into question our being.

It is not the other way around, as Nietzsche and Feuerbach would have it. The overwhelming experience of humankind is just this: when we come face to face with the divine, it is *our* reality that no longer seems so solid; God's reality is beyond question. "No man may look on my face for he will surely die."

History and the Glory of God

Is there any way in the world, then, that we can know anything at all about God?

The next part of the story fills in the content between the brackets. God sets Moses beside him on a rock—in the cleft of a rock. "And while my glory passes by," he said, "I will cover you with my hand until I have passed by; then I will take away my hand, and you shall see my back; but my face shall not be seen."

For Israel this became the picture of how God revealed himself not only to Moses, but to them in their national history. God is not seen directly ("my face shall not be seen"), but indirectly in the events of history. Some have suggested, with much merit I believe, that God is most often known only after the event ("you shall see my back"), only after he has performed his work. Then, in reflecting on that event, people come to know that God was in it all along.

essay

In the midst of the desert, the people of Israel complained against Moses, chafed at their discomfort and fell into rebellion against God. This they did while miracles abounded, while the columns of cloud and fire led them, while they had the fresh memory of a miraculous escape from Pharaoh's army. Only later did these events come back to them, and they realized that here, here and here were the evidences of God in their midst. Only a very human trait allows even wonders to become commonplace while we are in the midst of them. How many extraordinary people have we only begun to appreciate when they are no longer with us? How often have travelers to foreign lands found themselves bored and disinterested among strange and wonderful sights, only to say later what a pity it was that they did not attend more carefully to every detail?

As a student reading Wordsworth's great ode "Intimations of Immortality from Recollections of Early Childhood," I had great difficulty in understanding the poem and rather doubted that there was any real substance to the words:

There was a time when meadow, grove and stream
The earth and every common sight,
   To me did seem
Apparelled in celestial light,
The glory and the freshness of a dream.

Now as I have grown older I read those words with the poignancy that comes from recognizing a common experience. But while I was young I did not understand these things, or see them quite this way. Then I lived in the atmosphere of that very feeling for life. I was perhaps, as Wordsworth incautiously describes the youth, "Nature's Priest." But I could hardly have realized that the emotions could be dulled, or that the sky, trees and "every common sight" could be experienced in any other way. Only with the change of season and climate do I finally realize the meaning of the poet's words when he said,

It is not now as it hath been of yore;
   Turn wheresoe'er I may
   By night or day
The things which I have seen
I now can see no more.

Maturity, of course, has its compensations. And the Spirit of God brings new experiences and more lasting affections. But everyone who has lived a certain number of years has at least experienced what Wordsworth describes. Few of us, however, appreciate the reality of these things until the experiences he describes have passed behind a curtain of years, never to be recovered in quite the same way that childhood and youth present them. But looking back, we can say, Ah yes! there is a certain quality about the sights and sounds of childhood, about the emotions of youth, that grows ever fainter with the years. Only in retrospect can we fully see that. As with so many significant events in life, only afterward do we realize that the very angels of God have stood in our midst and the power of his Spirit worked mightily among us.

The Rock of History
But there is another thing here, something we dare not miss.

God had said, in effect, that the intensity of his glory would consume man, and that man cannot stand and look on God directly. Yet, he answered Moses' request in a remarkable manner. While he *shielded* him from his glory, he still *surrounded* him with his glory. He passed by, and Moses saw him receding; but he had come so close to the center of God's power, so suffused was the atmosphere of that encounter, that Moses himself was changed. The brightness of his own face had to be veiled from the people at the foot of the mountain. The encounter had been indirect; he was hid within the cleft of the rock. But the indirectness of God's encounter with Moses was more direct and intense than the experience of any other being.

So it is that John said of the Christ: "We have beheld his glory, glory as of the only Son from the Father. . . . And from his fulness have we all received, grace upon grace" (Jn 1:14, 16). The intensity and the reality of the experience was unparalleled. Yet even here, John must say, "No one has ever seen God; the only Son, who is in the bosom of the Father, he has made him known" (v. 18). Jesus was, as the great old hymn says, "the Rock of Ages cleft for me." It was through his history, his story, that we are thrust into the midst of God's surrounding glory, yet shielded by the indirectness of that very history.

Thus the incarnation of God in Christ presents, in a more intense form, what the Bible claimed to say about God all along. "In many and various ways," the writer of Hebrews said, "God spoke of old to our fathers by the prophets." But now the incarnate Christ "reflects the glory of God and bears the very stamp of his nature."

It Makes a Difference

Growing up in the South I learned to say Sir and Ma'am to my elders and people in authority. It was a form of address that I never dreamed would be considered "quaint" or "overpolite" in other parts of the country. I still prefer it, but it took getting outside of my accustomed environment to understand the uniqueness of habits with which I had grown up.

What I have said so far about the Christian faith can look altogether common and normal until we see these features alongside the whole panorama and history of religious thought. Then they stand out from the background of world religions because of the brilliant uniqueness of the insights they hold.

The broader history of world religious thought has yielded two other ways that man has typically found his clues in trying to work out the puzzle of life. One way is to identify ultimate meaning (divinity) with nature itself; the other way has been to look within or beyond nature, for a deeper unity of all things. Either of these stands in surprising contrast to what I have been saying about biblical religion.

The Religion of Nature
To explain the mystery of life, one might look at the multitude of natural objects and events all around him. This is the more primitive route to a religious expression of life.

Through the ages before Christianity, and to a significant extent even after the advent of the Christian faith, religious knowledge has sprung from the observation of nature. Myth ties the phenomena together, giving them a coherent explanation. The sun and the stars, riverbeds and forests, are saturated with power and significance.

Nature is understood concretely as the medium of the divine. To understand the gods, then, one attends to the regular patterns of nature, with its cycles, its decay and disorder, its fertility and new birth. Every event yields to mythological explanation. Every chance occurrence invites, in fact demands, a response. Every new season, each new year, the end of every lunar cycle calls for prodigious efforts. Even our Christmas celebration is built on a pagan rite whose original intention was to overturn the cycle of events leading to longer and longer nights with consequent shorter days. Great efforts were needed to gain longer days, before the sun ceased to shine entirely.

Deities, spirits and invisible powers occupy every corner of the landscape. They must be satisfied with food, music, libations and sacrifice; sometimes they are given shelter. In Taiwan, I was walking along a riverbank with a group of Chinese students. Suddenly we came upon a small temple, only a little larger than a doghouse. "What is this?" I asked. They explained that at a river bend there was always the danger that the spirit of the river would run over the bank, missing the sharp turn in the river. Then this ghost would wander around the neighborhood causing mischief. Therefore this house is provided for him, so he will have a place to stay at rest.

That is a popular explanation, but the point is easy to see. Nature and the divine are one and the same. The operation of nature is the operation of the divine.

In this view, the power of a divine being is sometimes limited by geographical space or by natural boundaries. In Old Testament history there is the story of Benhadad's invasion of Israel with his Syrian army. Benhadad was soundly defeated. His advisers, however, analyzed their defeat this way: "Their gods are gods of the hills, and so they were stronger than we; but let us fight against them in the plain, and surely we shall be stronger than they" (1 Kings 20:23). The ancient Syrians, along with others who maintain a "natural" religion, saw the world as a patchwork of powers. Nature demonstrates many different forces, and they all have to be reckoned with. The possibility of a unity within the world, among people or within nature does not suggest itself in the religions of nature: there is only the great diversity of powers.

The gods of Syria and the gods of other nations are not the same. Neither people nor the earth itself possesses the basis of unity. That had to wait for an idea—more than an idea, an experience!—that was held, against great odds, by a few prophetic figures in an obscure nation in a small corner of the Mediterranean world. It had to wait for the Israelite obsession with the idea that there is only *one* supreme power in all of the universe, that all things are completely dependent upon that power, for there is only *one* God, the creator and sustainer of all that exists. That obsession, that conviction—that notion held for so long by a tiny minority of humankind—was, of course, carried to the world by the Christian movement. But in the religions of nature, with their basic assumptions, that supreme conviction is not possible.

One other point needs to be made about the religions of nature. It is important in seeing the difference between this style of thought and that of the Jews and Christians. The point is this: the view of the world as a patchwork of powers, as a diversity of being, is supported by the notion that nothing really new ever happens. History is merely the working out of the various potentialities of nature. The cycles of birth, growth, maturity and death continue without any major change. Seasons come and go; years measure the greater cycles of a cosmic timetable. Thus the more things change, the more they remain the same.

In the Bible we have a remnant of this kind of thinking in the melancholy thesis of Ecclesiastes:

What has been is what will be,
  and what has been done is what
    will be done;
  and there is nothing new under
    the sun.
Is there a thing of which it is said,
  "See, this is new"?
It has been already,
  in the ages before us. (Eccles 1:9-10)

Hardly a typical thought for the Old Testament, as Ecclesiastes in fact is an atypical book, yet it serves to set in relief the Bible's insistence on a quite different view of God in his relation to the world.

Religion beyond Nature

The second possible basis for religious thought is what Will Herberg called "Greek-Oriental spirituality," because of a basic agreement between Greek philosophy and Oriental mysticism. That agreement, simply stated, is that there is a hidden unity within nature that emerges in the forms and events of the visible world. This view of the world is different from the religion of nature in that here there *is* the possibility of unity. At its basis, everything comes together in an undifferentiated unity, and the pilgrimage of the mind or the soul is one that tends toward the discovery of that unity.

In another important way, however, it maintains something in common with the religions of nature. Namely, neither of them expects anything new. Reality is a static reality. All events, all thought, all expectations, are nothing more than the outworking of an eternal potentiality. "There is nothing new under the sun." All possibilities are simply the repeated themes of a forgotten past. The arena of human life is a closed circle; run as fast as you might, you will never escape.

A young Chinese woman, the daughter of a fisherman, wrote me about her desire to go to seminary and be trained as a Christian worker. Ellen (her adopted English name) belonged to a family that still held to the traditional animist beliefs, with a strong mixture of Buddhism. Her father simply could not believe or understand his daughter's search for a new kind of life. "This is just for foreigners, not for fish country," he would say. Here is a blend of the two possibilities that I have mentioned—animism and Buddhism, a religion of nature and a religion beyond nature. Neither of these provide the basis for understanding new events or new possibilities.

These two ways of thinking, the religions of nature and Greek-Oriental spirituality, cover almost all of the options except those that have come directly or indirectly from the Judeo-Christian tradition. Intellectually these former options can be quite satisfying, because what our rational faculties strive for is a closed system, one in which the pieces of the puzzle fit, the nexus is shut tight, and there are no openings into a beyond that cannot be explained. That is a basic urge in our mental processes, because the purpose of our rational intellect is to give order to the world we live in, and mystery threatens that order.

That is why a modern phenomenon that might be called "scientism" or naturalism—not true science, but the notion espoused by people like Carl Sagan that science holds the key to all the mysteries of life—actually fits into these earlier nonhis-

torical views of life. I think science itself is tending to confirm
the Judeo-Christian model of reality as history, and not as a
static, closed system. It is not science itself, but the exaggerated
claims that are made for science that I have in mind when I
say that it begins to fit well into the category of the religion of
nature. Or, when they look for a deeper rational unity of all
things, it reminds one of the Greek-Oriental spirituality. In either case, there is the idea that all answers will emerge out of the
universe as it is: there is nothing new, no innovation, no un-
expected turns that will break the static pattern of reality.

The point at which that kind of prejudice stops, of course, is
at the point of a real beginning of something, or a real end.
It is stumped by crisis, by a sudden mutation and by any substantial change that causes life really to be different. For all of
its glibness in the everyday course of events, it suddenly is
struck dumb at the contemplation of the beginning of the universe—or by the thought of its end. Why is there something,
rather than nothing? Scientism, no less than the religions of
nature, has nothing to say. Both of them must begin with an
eternal substance. Only a religion of history can afford the
luxurious simplicity of a creation—out of nothing! Above all,
these thinkers who insist on the impossibility of innovation—
real innovation that is—are positively undone by the prospects
suggested by the resurrection: *novo creatio ex nihilo!*

Reality and History

I have said that the other ways of viewing the world are intellectually satisfying. That is a bit of an exaggeration, but it is
basically true because the intellect strives after order and will
sometimes be satisfied if it can be presented with a pattern,
even if that pattern doesn't exactly fit reality.

But if they are intellectually or rationally satisfying, they still
do not satisfy a fundamental need of the human psyche. That
is, the soul longs for purpose, for a direction in life. That need
is described in the very human quality of *hope*. Our lives are
inevitably oriented toward the future; there is a longing for
something—something that we do not altogether understand.

C. S. Lewis was attracted to the German term *Sehnsucht* which described this feeling: it is a longing for something we know should be there but is not yet present—a homesickness for heaven.

History is history because events are perceived as moving toward a goal. It is not *simply* moving from one innovation to another—that would indeed be a tiresome sort of variety. But it is a moving toward something—something that utterly sums up and makes sense of all the scattered tragic and heroic events of the past.

This goal orientation of the Bible is clear enough. The whole text is stamped with a hope in future fulfillment. The Pentateuch (the first five books of the Old Testament) speaks of a promised land, one that stands at the end of the wilderness wanderings. The prophets speak of a new messianic age in which "nation shall not lift up sword against nation," of a new kingdom and a new Jerusalem. The New Testament speaks of the kingdom of God.

The psychological and social power of this attraction toward a goal should be abundantly clear to twentieth-century people. It is in our century that secular mass movements, such as Nazism and Marxist-Leninism, have moved masses basically on the strength of a pirated Christian view of history. The kingdom of God has been changed, in those versions, to a Thousand Year Reich or a Realm of Freedom, but they gain their power from that great subliminal urge that all people share for a "house made not with hands, eternal in heaven" and for a time in which God becomes "all and in all."

History and the Holy Spirit

One other point needs to be stressed, lest I give the impression that God is revealing himself through some impersonal process of history. This indeed is how some, such as Hegel, have turned around the Christian understanding of history. In this case, we view ourselves as standing off remotely surveying the panorama of history and coming to a conclusion about what it all means. This was precisely the case with the ancient gnostic heresy: it was turning the gospel of love into a possession of the intellect. History is the medium of God's self-revelation; but the initiate into this kind of knowledge (gnosis) is not a part of that history, this knowledge excludes risks and crises, possibility and promise. It excludes the need for faith—for those things that are seen clearly no longer require faith. In other words, this other view of history (even though it includes God's self-disclosure) refuses personal involvement and trust, which are always the most important elements of faith.

When we say that God reveals himself in history and that this is the biblical perspective, we have to mean something quite different. The difference is this: the understanding of what God does, or has done, in history is made possible through his personal encounter with a man or woman of faith. To Moses God responds to the request to reveal his *ways* by saying, "This very thing . . . I will do; for you have found favor in my sight, and *I know you by name*" (Ex 33:17). In the New Testament, this specifically is an office of the Holy Spirit, who now makes the presence of God available to all who believe: "The Counselor, the Holy Spirit, whom the Father will send in my name, he will teach you all things, and bring to your remembrance all that I have said to you" (Jn 14:26).

The history of the Old and New Testaments, then, as important as it is for understanding the biblical view of God, is not a great drama to which Christians become spectators. The one element absolutely essential in this history is the personal involvement of the believer. The drama is one, as Kierkegaard suggested, in which we are suddenly transfixed by the main actor, who is also the director. He steps to the front of the stage, points his finger and calls out, "You, you're wanted. Come up here. Take your part!"

Now it becomes not only history, but salvation history. That is why biblical history, which is absolutely foundational to biblical thinking, is never written as if to an impartial observer. The history of the Bible is, without apology, an appeal, an invitation—and a promise.

3
The Role
of Faith in
Bible Reading

———

In Murphy, North Carolina—my wife's hometown—the story has circulated for years about a certain congregation in that mountain region who decided to sell their property and build on a new site. They found a buyer and everything seemed in order until they discovered that the deed, written way back in the pioneer beginnings of that church, was made out to "the Lord God Almighty." They consulted a lawyer to find out how in heaven's name they could transfer the deed. He puzzled over it for some time. Finally, one day he met a county judge on the streets of Murphy and asked how he thought the problem should be handled.

"It's really very simple," said the judge. "Run an announcement in the paper stating the church's intentions and that, if the owner still has an interest in this property, he must make it known. Then, after a reasonable time, run another announcement that 'After thorough and diligent search, God Almighty cannot be found in Cherokee County, North Carolina, and the disposal of this property devolves to the deacons of said church.' "

However apocryphal this story might be, it points up something that the biblical writers dealt with continually. The fact is that apart from the eyes of faith God may well appear to be altogether absent from Cherokee County, North Carolina—or from anywhere else in this world.

In the preceding chapter I attempted to point out that the Hebrews and the later Christians saw history as the medium in which God made himself known. But the minute I say that, further explanation is required. Because history—any history at all—is not simply the bare facts of what happened at a particular time in a particular place. What constitutes the history of the United States is not just a list of events that happened over the last two centuries within our borders. Not only would such a catalog be sterile and boring, but it would not really be history. History requires that someone say, "This is the significant common experience of a people." Some events, greatly touted and hailed at the time, prove to be of little consequence in the long run; others, that seemed unportentous at the time, have great significance because of their long-term effect on many further developments.

In 1801 the Supreme Court was considered a body of such little importance that President Adams had difficulty filling the post of chief justice. Each appointment was refused. Finally, without knowing where else to turn, he nominated his own secretary of state, John Marshall. The event was considered to be of little consequence at the time. But the history of our American judicial system dates from that appointment of the "father of judicial review." To us, that was a tremendously significant event: to the people of the time, it was among the less distinguished appointments made by the second president of the young national government. What was required, in order to give that event its proper significance, was the perspective gained by later experiences.

Abraham, the patriarch, was hardly distinguished from a thousand other semitic traders who wandered back and forth across the frontier borders of Egypt. The great Middle Kingdom celebrated its triumphs and suffered its disasters; it marked with huge stone obelisks its greatness and its supremacy over lesser nations. Little note would have been given to Abraham. Yet today the great and the near-great of Egypt's Middle Kingdom are all but forgotten, while the name of Abraham is known to millions upon millions some 4000 years after he lived. The difference? A perception that transcends the preoccupations of an era. It is a perception that holds that some events, little noted at the time, are of signal importance in the providential design of God. To that kind of insight, an insight guided and energized by faith, Abraham's small choices in life were of enormously greater importance than the titanic struggles and the celebrated triumphs of an empire.

Therefore, no history is self-evident. Nothing could be more false than the saying, "Let the facts speak for themselves": they don't. History is, in one sense perhaps, a series of events—it has its objective and factual element. But these events of the past must be ordered in our minds and perceived according to certain principles.

More particularly, the history through which God reveals himself, and which is the subject of the biblical witness, is history as perceived by men and women of faith. It is so ordered, and it is given its peculiar significance, because in these events believers have perceived the very hand of God. The eyes of the faithful have seen the events in the life of Christ, for instance, and said, "Thou art the Christ." Or they have said, "Truly this man was the Son of God." It is important to note, however, that others saw the same events and said: "He casts out demons by the power of Beelzebub"; or "If you are the Christ, give us a sign"; or any number of other comments that tells us not everyone saw the same events in the same light. Almost everyone saw the crucifixion as the end of the story for Jesus, as a positive repudiation of all he had taught about himself. Subsequent events, however, caused Jesus' disciples to look back on those same events and see that they meant something very different.

Faith and Reliable History
What is it, however, that keeps faith from being a purely arbitrary reading of history? Well over a century ago, Søren Kier-

kegaard remarked that "what modern philosophy understands by faith is what properly is called an opinion, or what is loosely called in everyday speech believing."[1]

An example that would conform to a popular understanding of faith comes from Lewis Carroll's *Through the Looking Glass*. Alice encounters the Queen, who tells her how old she is:

"Just one hundred and one, five months and a day."

"I can't believe that," said Alice.

"Can't you?" the Queen said with a pitying tone. "Try again; draw a long breath, and shut your eyes."

Alice coughed. "There's no use trying," she said, "one can't believe impossible things."

"I daresay you haven't had much practice," said the Queen.[2]

If this were faith, then it would make a shambles and a fraud of any Christian understanding of history. Taken in its biblical sense, faith is a reliable and consistent way of seeing and understanding things. It is not arbitrary belief or a hardheaded clinging to doctrine, but it is something else, something altogether more disciplined and reliable.

Two features mark the character of biblical faith:

1. *Faith is a perception that proves itself reliable.* It is "the assurance of things hoped for, the conviction of things not seen" (Heb 11:1).

In our building there hangs a large woodcut design that is made up of a strange swirling combination of dark and light patches. To the uninitiated it looks like a maze with no real pattern at all. To others it presents a picture of Christ. But once you have seen the image of Christ in the pattern, you have difficulty knowing how you ever missed it. Every time you look, there is the image of Christ, as plain as the nose on your face. In a similar way the Bible teaches us to see history through eyes of faith. Once we see it that way, it is not a peculiar and idiosyncratic way of perceiving things; it proves to be a reliable way of seeing the world. Faith has not fashioned a pattern where there was none, but it has shown us a pattern that is always there.

2. *Faith involves more than intellectual assent; it requires an assent of the whole personality—emotions, will and intellect.* "By faith we understand that the world was created by the word of God" (Heb 11:3)—that involves the intellect. "By faith Abel offered to God a more acceptable sacrifice" (v. 4); "By faith Abraham obeyed" (v. 8); "by faith he sojourned" (v. 9); "By faith Abraham, when he was tested, offered up Isaac" (v. 17); "By faith the people crossed the Red Sea as if on dry land" (v. 29)—these are all actions and involve the will. By faith Abraham "looked forward to the city which has foundations, whose builder and maker is God" (v. 10); many died in faith who "desire a better country, that is, a heavenly one" (v. 16)—these involve intuitive and emotional faculties. Faith involves the investment of all that is in us.

A famous high-wire walker visited the Talulah Gorge in the north Georgia mountains. He was to walk across a cable that had been stretched across that great chasm, with its white-water river appearing as a small ribbon at the bottom of the gorge. At first, so the story has been told, the acrobat called out to the crowd, "Do you believe I can do it?"

"Yes," they shouted, "go ahead—you can do it!"

He jumped down from his perch and wrestled a wheelbarrow into position on the wire cable. Once again he challenged them, "Do you believe I can push this wheelbarrow all the way across to the other side?"

"Yes, we believe: do it!"

Having the crowd in his spell, he singled out a young man in his early twenties. "Do you believe, young man, that I can get this wheelbarrow all the way across?"

"Of course, you can do it," was the young man's spirited reply.

"Are you sure?"

"Of course!"

"All right," said the acrobat to his young enthusiast, "come up and get in the wheelbarrow."

Faith, you see, is altogether more than intellectual confidence.

Scripture as a Dialog of Faith

Habakkuk made an important discovery as he puzzled over a question—an acutely troubling and seemingly unanswerable question. The question arose from the fact that, even though he knew the nation of Judah to be wicked, the Babylonians were undoubtedly more wicked. Why then would a just and holy God allow Babylon to profit while it swallowed up a nation more righteous than they? Habakkuk eventually arrived at an answer. The end of the matter had not yet been seen. The tale was not fully told: God would prove to be just in the final analysis, even though at the time the scales were not balanced.

The prophet then brought his argument to a resolution: God is faithful—therefore, those who are righteous shall live by being faithful. "The righteous," Habakkuk said, "shall live by his faith" (Hab 2:4). The focus is on the conviction that God will perform and bring to completion his intention: man's moral response is based on the faithfulness of God.

When Paul used that same verse, quoting it in Romans (1:17), he focuses on our response. If we believe that God is faithful, then we shall live, and live righteously, in the light of that faith.

In other words, both sides of the matter are emphasized. Habakkuk stressed God's faithfulness to his promise—that is objective, and it is demonstrated in the course of events. Paul stressed the human, subjective appropriation of that promise: it is the disposition of the will and the emotion and the intellect. Both the objective and the subjective sides are necessary. God speaks indirectly through history. We listen, aided by the predisposition to hear what God has to say. Faith-history, which is the history to which Scripture refers, is a dialog between God and humankind.

A Clue for Reading Scripture

This realization of how Scripture relates to faith-history gives us an enormously important clue about how we should read and understand Scripture. In the first place it helps us get past a common misconception that is positively disastrous to anyone who seriously wants to understand Scripture.

For some strange reason quite well-read and intelligent people are constantly speaking of the Bible as if it were a collection of simple declarative statements. Whether critics or defenders of the Bible, they insist on referring to it as if it were a great deposit of straightforward maxims on this subject or that.

Upon actually reading the Bible, however, what these same people would find is that some few books—like Proverbs, for instance—fit that description, but most do not. And some, like Ecclesiastes or Job, for example, are just the opposite. What they would find, upon reading the whole of the Bible, is that it contains not only statements declaring what is true but questions. Not only that, it raises doubts. And it voices complaints. It speaks with awe and wonder. So, far from showing the stamp of certitude, it often shows writers who are overwhelmed with the mystery of life, the majesty of God and the power of the Spirit.

Sometimes it speaks vividly and descriptively of the future—an example would be in 2 Thessalonians or (making allowances for the symbolism) the Revelation. At other times it only questions the future, and the sufficient answer, in Habakkuk for instance, is "the righteous shall live by faithfulness." Sometimes it proclaims the rule that those who live faithfully will find God's reward. Proverbs and Deuteronomy state that great principle. At other times, however, it questions that rule and wonders why the righteous suffer while the wicked appear to live sumptuously and respectably. Job takes us down that path.

The Bible and the Koran: The Great Contrast
All of this should warn us that the Bible's way of getting at the truth is not quite the same as the copybook maxims of years ago. The Islamic view of the Koran provides a striking contrast to the Christian view of the Scriptures that helps set in relief what I am attempting to describe.

Muhammad, the great prophet of Islam, is supposed to have received the Koran in a series of revelations. He was simply the conduit through which the words of Allah were received and transmitted. The Koran, in contrast to the Bible, is a book of direct statements on various subjects purporting to be divinely revealed.

Now, in contrast to Islam's scripture, one can see just how different the Christian idea of Scripture has been—from the very earliest times when these books were first considered to be canon. For what we have revealed in the Bible is not only, in such a direct sense, *what* God said, but the *way* in which he revealed himself. That also is an aspect of the Word. God revealed himself to men and women, in a wide variety of circumstances.

The Bible often includes both sides of the conversation. We see God in the light of human questioning and human need. And we also see men and women in the light of God's judgment, mercy and love. The Hebrew prophets not only spoke for God, but they lived lives seeking after God: their faith and the history of their faith are a part of what is revealed.

Suppose a man tells you of a beautiful woman he has met and with whom he has fallen in love. He describes her appearance, how she talks, what she says. He enumerates her better qualities: she is self-confident; she has a sense of humor; she is also quite intelligent and very popular. He has told you something about this woman, and you listen with a mild degree of interest.

But suppose he tells you how ardently he has sought after her, how he had agonized when it seemed he had lost her, how diligently he has pursued her affection. And what sacrifices he has made! More than once he has reformed bad habits. He has worked hard to convince her that he is a man on his way up. From a cavalier young man without serious intention, he has become purposeful, serious and even ambitious. Her affection has filled him with joy: it has given him a new regard for himself, and it has given him new insight into the subtleties of love between a man and a woman. That tells us infinitely more than the first, rather straightforward, account.

The revelation embodied in our Scripture, in a similar way, encompasses much more than a transmission from heaven. It takes in more than God's answers to the prophets, it also includes their questions, their longings, the doubts that plagued them. The prophet's word, for instance, is the word of God not simply because of what has been said, but because of what has happened in the prophet's life. Not only is it God objectively acting in the world, but it is man responding to God. What we have revealed to us is not just the bare word of the prophet, but his *life*.

Doubting Prophets, Doubting Saints

Now I want to drive that point just a bit further.

The Bible is a book of faith, but not precisely because it urges us on to belief. It does that much, but it also does quite a lot more: for instance, it speaks frankly and openly about doubt. And when it speaks of faith, seldom does it have the same ring as an Easy Piety which says, "Always believe, and never for a moment doubt, and everything will turn out for the best."

If the Bible provides a grammar of faith, it is hard for some to believe that doubt is a part of that grammar. You can easily get the impression in some circles that doubt is to be avoided like the plague if one is serious about religion. I am not at all certain where anyone would arrive at that notion, but I am fairly certain you would not get it from reading Scripture.

What we are forced to see, if we actually read Scripture, is that doubt is not foreign at all to the writers. Part of what has driven them into real and deep conversation with God is their profoundly disturbing questions. The result is that doubt and despair, though they are not the end and goal of Scripture, actually play a remarkably prominent role in the progress of that conversation which leads to faith.

No modern existentialist has posed the dilemma of existence in a more serious and devastating form than have the prophets. None of the modern anti-theists, whether Nietzsche or Feuerbach, whether Marx or Comte, have leveled questions about the love or the justice of God in any way more serious in their intent than has the writer of Job or Ecclesiastes. If Camus is rightly credited with having said that suicide is the only real philosophical question, his despair is in every way anticipated by Jeremiah:

> Cursed be the day on which I was born!
> The day when my mother bore me, let it not be blessed!
> Cursed be the man who brought the news to my father,
>   "A son is born to you," making him very glad.
> Why did I come forth from the womb to see toil and sorrow,
>   and spend my days in shame? (Jer 20:14-15, 18)

Few pronounce that kind of despair more convincingly than Job:

> Let the day perish wherein I was born,
>   and the night which said,
>   "A man-child is conceived."
> Let that day be darkness!
>   May God above not seek it,
>   nor light shine upon it.
> Let gloom and deep darkness claim it.
>   Let clouds dwell upon it;
>   let the blackness of the day terrify it. . . .
>   Because it did not shut the doors of my mother's womb,
>   nor hide trouble from my eyes.
> Why did I not die at birth,
>   come forth from the womb and expire? (Job 3:3-5, 10-11)

Of the advantage of death over life, Job says:

> There the wicked cease from troubling,
>   and there the weary are at rest.
> There the prisoners are at ease together;
>   they hear not the voice of the taskmaster.
> The small and the great are there,
>   and the slave is free from his master. (Job 3:17-19)

Why, then, is life given to those who would so benefit from an early death? Some there are, like himself, who would long for it and "dig for it more than for hid treasures" (v. 21). Remember that Job's tormentor (Satan) is permitted to afflict him in any way short of taking his life. In this extremity Job is brought to the point of questioning "Why life rather than death?" In this form, the question becomes the ultimate expression of doubt—not only the questioning of all things but also the questioning of the meaning of all things.

To these examples a great deal more could be added. Perhaps most significant is the one book in the Old Testament that stands as a great question mark in the midst of the Old Testament faith—Ecclesiastes. With the exception of the last verse or so, that is practically all it is. Having examined all matters for which men strive—wisdom, wealth, pleasure—the preacher pronounces that all things are like a vapor that disappears as soon as it is seen. All is vanity. Therefore he said, "I hated life, because what is done under the sun was grievous to me; for all is vanity and a striving after wind" (Eccles 2:17).

These are not straw men that biblical writers have set up in order to destroy them with an easy faith. They have no apologies to make to a Montaigne or a Nietzsche or a Camus concerning the strength of their questions or the potency of their doubts. But there is something, an extra energy in this doubt of theirs, something qualitatively different from the doubt of the skeptic, or the hidden doubt of the timid and fearful believer. In the hands of the presumptuous skeptic it becomes a dead end, something that dissolves relationships and abandons hope. It is the last thing before madness; just as Nietzsche's *The Anti-Christ* was the last essay in the twilight of his sanity. Likewise, to the believer who fears losing his fragile faith, doubt is debilitating, paralyzing.

What was so different about the doubts of Jeremiah? Here was one of the greatest prophets of Israel, ranked with Isaiah and Ezekiel, and with a more difficult message to pronounce than either of these others. Yet here was a prophet whose doubts plumbed the very depths of the human soul. Why was I born? he asked. God is stronger than me, and he has taken advantage of my weakness. No one listens or takes heed, yet God has made it such that I cannot cease from speaking—it is as if a fire were pent up in my bones and I am compelled to speak (Jer 20).

His doubts, in fact, were not answered as his career progressed—they were intensified. Look at his early career: there he championed the reform of Josiah. God was moving in those days to restore the law and the priesthood, to lift up the temple as the central shrine of worship. At considerable personal risk, Jeremiah pressed for the reform.

And the reform was successful. The "high places," so tainted with idolatrous pagan associations, were abandoned and the temple cult at Jerusalem spoke in a way more pure and unde-filed of the Lord of Israel. All was well. God had triumphed; his will was established; his able king was on the throne.

Then, suddenly, it all became as a dream that had vanished. Josiah was slain in the valley of Megiddo, where he had fool-ishly attempted to prevent the Egyptian army from marching north. With Josiah went the reform. First the Egyptians and then the Babylonians enforced their dominance over Judah. Soon the city of Jerusalem was besieged by the mighty army of Nebuchadnezzar. By 587, the temple had been destroyed.

Through all of this, what had happened to the conviction that God was responsible for the reforms of Josiah? Why these strange reversals that made all their former labors and sacrific-es vain? Only as Jeremiah stands amid the rubble of these former convictions, plagued with doubt, do we discover those utterances that distinguish this prophet from all of the others that Israel produced. Only because he faced the dilemma and asked the difficult questions could he later see that even if God had willed the reforms of Josiah, and even if he desired to establish a purer and holier temple worship, his greatest will went even further.

The temple and the priestly cult were visible symbols of some-thing much deeper and more lasting—something that could never be destroyed and that was in no way affected by the operations of foreign oppressors. Here was the essential matter all along. But only as Jeremiah turned to face those circumstanc-es that mocked his faith did they become apparent. Only now could he say:

> Behold, the days are coming, says the LORD, when I will make a new covenant with the house of Israel and the house of Judah, not like the covenant which I made with their fathers. . . . But this is the covenant . . . I will put my law

within them, and I will write it upon their hearts; and will be
their God, and they shall be my people. (Jer 31:31-33)

Faith: The Key to Bible Study
We must take our clues on how to read the Bible from how the
Bible is written. There is nothing here, for instance, to suggest
that we should suspend our critical judgment so that we are not
troubled by doubts. Jeremiah didn't; nor should we.

Nevertheless, although reading the Bible in the light of faith
does not imply less than critical judgment, it does imply more.
If it is by faith that we read, then in addition to the intellect,
we also involve our emotions and will.

It is not altogether unlike a man who is reasonably prudent
in his intentions to marry. He thinks critically about the practical aspects of marriage. He considers how to make the marriage financially secure. He takes into account what common
interests, what likes and dislikes he would find in the woman
he is to marry. He compares their religious persuasions and
even their political loyalties. He notes how they each spend
their money, and how they spend their time. But when he falls
in love and proposes marriage, he does not hold before his
mental eye a checklist entitled The Marriageable Woman, or
anything of that sort. No, he leads with his emotions and his
will, though his intellect may give its consent. He, in fact, abandons the pursuit of intellectual certainty for the sake of discovering more completely the mystery of that other person.

The Bible is a book that draws on personal involvement. It
makes demands on the entire personality. If we cannot read
Jeremiah sympathetically, then we cannot understand him well.
If we are not willing to believe that John has experienced a
living God, then his many words about love fail to touch us. The
Bible becomes most fully known and most completely ours only
when we are willing to risk ourselves to it.

In this connection it is important to see that the man who
proposes marriage has not forgone his practical questions for
the sake of knowing less, but in order to know more. For all of
his practical questions on the feasibility of marriage, before he

knew it he was at the point where mental effort would take him no further. If he wanted to know more—and by this time he did so passionately—then he could only proceed by taking a risk. He must trust his intuition, and he must plunge ahead by the power of his emotions and will. Only then will experience prove what he hopes with all his heart is true. Thus it is also true that the Bible cannot yield all that it has to give without the risk of wholehearted personal involvement—without the risk that we call faith.

But this abandonment of ourselves to the Word of God—like the abandonment to the risk of marriage—is a proper method only because of the nature of the engagement. We engage the Bible at a personal level because it is a distinctly personal book. That we come to know God in a personal way is, of course, the central aim. But we are drawn all the closer to that aim because the Bible's message is inseparable from the personalities of its writers and major figures, and from their human experience of God.

The Bible is a book of faith that responds to faith, because it does not simply reveal *things about God.* And it is not simply a message delivered through whatever human instrument was at hand, whose name and personality is inconsequential. Instead it yields itself to faith because, as much as the message, it is the messenger that comes into view. We come to know the writer's own peculiar experience of life, what has caused him pain and what has been his delight, what preoccupies his mind and what engages his affections. We come to know his will and his sentiment, without which his dogma is barren and spiritless. We follow his doubts until they issue in faith. If faith comes hard to him, then we understand all the more his experience, because it might come hard to us as well.

So, surrounded by the full scope of human experience—with Sarah we laugh, with David we have remorse, with Peter our confidence evaporates at the crucial moment, with Paul we feel ourselves the chief of sinners—we are led as full human beings into the presence of God.

PART II
The Practice
of Bible
Reading

The point of this section is to straighten out a few curves and avoid an unnecessary cul-de-sac often found in even the most well-planned approaches to Bible study. First, we must keep in mind from the beginning where we intend to go. It is remarkable how some advanced planning with a map will save hours of time on the road. In the same way, I am convinced that what it takes to save many well-intentioned journeys into Scripture is a plan that envisions the points of destination along the route.

Along with that it must be simple. It could almost be stated as an axiom: The more complicated our method for studying the Bible, the more superficial the results. The corollary to that can be taken too far, but I think it is more than fair to say that if a plan is simple and purposeful it will yield the greatest benefits to students of the Bible.

4
A Whole-
Bible
Strategy

Modern Bible study at almost every level of interest, from
the university and seminary to the Sunday-school classroom,
suffers from a fundamental lapse. Professor Richard G. Moul-
ton long ago made an intriguing comment on this painfully
obvious state of affairs that is surprisingly up-to-date:

> We have done almost everything that is possible with these
> Hebrew and Greek writings. We have overlaid them, clause
> by clause, with exhaustive commentaries; we have translated
> them, revised the translations, and quarrelled over the revi-
> sions; we have discussed authenticity and inspiration, and
> suggested textual history with colored type; we have mechan-
> ically divided the whole into chapters and verses, and sought
> texts to memorize and quote; we have epitomized into hand-
> books and extracted school lessons; we have recast from the
> feminine point of view, and even from the standpoint of the
> next century. There is yet one thing left to do with the Bible:
> simply to read it.[1]

And that is just the deficiency that we should first want to
remedy. It has seemed to me that a great weakness of introductory Bible study in many colleges and seminaries has been their

tendency to reach into the latest critical scholarship before students have properly acquainted themselves with the text itself. No wonder such efforts are often construed as "picking the Bible apart," when there is no real effort to see the Bible whole, as it stands. One needs to see the Parthenon from a respectful distance, to see it as a whole in all of its grandeur, before one inspects the mislaid stones, the joints in the columns and other timeworn features that become apparent with close examination. Biblical criticism—as valuable and constructive as much of it is—needs to be seen against the background of the full grandeur and beauty of the finished work.

D. L. Moody once invited his good friend Henry Drummond to speak at an American Chautauqua. Drummond at first declined, saying, "You don't want me to speak at your Chautauqua; I believe in three Isaiahs!" "That's all right," replied Moody. "You'll be speaking to people who don't even know there is *one* Isaiah." Our first task is to become acquainted with the text as it stands.

How to Get an Overview of the Bible

This section might be subtitled "Even if you know next to nothing about the Bible." Even those more experienced, I have found, need to know how to review basics. So we begin at the bottom of the ladder and progress rung by rung to the upper reaches of this world's most sublime and useful endeavor.

Martin Luther was one who knew how to place the Bible at the center of a Christian movement. He knew the Bible, he valued it, and there was nothing he was more serious about than teaching Christians how to study the Bible. He compared his method of studying the Bible to gathering apples from an apple tree. First, he said, he would lay hold of the trunk, shake it and collect the fruit that falls to the ground. Then he would climb into the tree and shake each of the larger branches separately. After that he would gather from each separate limb. Then he would inspect each twig. And finally he would look under each leaf to see what else could be found.[2]

That tells us, in a broad sense, how to begin. The first step is to lay hold of the great trunk of the apple tree and shake the whole tree. The *whole* Bible needs to be the first object of our consideration. We need to see it as a unity, with a great central theme and a simple sublime hope, giving witness in an intricately interwoven pattern to one God, one created order and to the essential unity of humankind.

Some people may immediately object that the Bible is not a book to be thought of as a whole, because it is a collection of books. They would be quite correct in emphasizing the fact that it is a collection, and a very diverse collection.

The name *Bible* applied to the single bound volume was not used until the fourth century. Even then, Chrysostom—who first used the term—designated this collection *Biblia,* a neuter plural, which was later mistaken for a feminine singular by the Western church and thus called by the singular noun *Bible.* By the church fathers it was often called a Divine Library. In England of 1516 the Bible was officially designated *Bibliotheca,* meaning library. So the Bible is not simply one volume but a collection that came together slowly and over a vast period of time. By most reckonings, the Bible is composed of sixty-six writings written over a period of at least twelve hundred years, by no fewer than forty-three authors.

Nevertheless, certain aspects of the Bible make it a whole and unified book. These aspects are sufficiently strong to justify our following Luther's suggestion of shaking the whole apple tree at once: it is not an orchard of separate, distinct and unrelated fruit trees, but a whole tree that branches out in differing directions. The limbs are quite separate, but they are all attached to the same trunk.

Without at all losing sight of the real and significant distinctions among the books, therefore, we need to recognize that they are more than just a collection of miscellaneous literature. They form a single and unique literature because they are recognized as having been written under the inspiration of the Holy Spirit, they bear the authority of God the Father, and they give true witness to God the Son. These writings, unlike any on earth, are peculiarly from God.

Furthermore, they are so recognized, in part, because all of
these various books bear a common theme. With unerring con-
sistency they all contribute to a nothing-less-than-astounding
pattern of thought concerning the relationship between God
and humanity. Like players of different instruments in an or-
chestra, their parts vary considerably, but the overall effect is
a symphony of divine purpose, whose theme again and again
is the redemption of humankind. Only by giving some consideration to the wholeness of the Bible can we see what the poet
Dryden recognized when he wrote:

Whence but from heaven could men unskilled in arts
In several ages born, in several parts,
Weave such agreeing truths, or how, or why
Should all conspire to cheat us with a lie?
Unasked their pains, ungrateful their advice,
Staying their gain, and martyrdom their price.

Even from a purely literary point of view, however, these books
belong together. They can be considered as a whole—if for no
other reason—because of the high degree of interdependence
among the writings. The messages of the prophets, for instance,
would be meaningless apart from the covenants recorded in
the books of the Law. Most of the books (apart from the wisdom
books of Job, Proverbs and Ecclesiastes) have in view the continual line of the history of early Israel. This history can be
understood by reading Genesis through Deuteronomy, followed by the books of Joshua, Judges, 1 and 2 Samuel and 1
and 2 Kings, and then 1 and 2 Chronicles, Ezra, and Nehemiah.
That history, in turn, is the indispensable background for an
accurate understanding of the New Testament. Even from a
secular level, then, the Bible exhibits a wholeness that must be
taken into consideration in any plan of study.

In addition to all of this, however, one other matter ought to
be emphasized. From the earliest beginnings of the Christian
movement—even before the New Testament was written or
collected—believers were impressed by a phenomenon that
was entirely unanticipated. It comes out in Luke's Gospel when
he tells the story of the Emmaus disciples. When these disciples

encountered the resurrected Christ, we read, he opened the Scriptures and "beginning with Moses and all the prophets, he interpreted to them in all the scriptures the things concerning himself" (Lk 24:27).

No one before had dared to propose that Scripture had a central figure. Abraham, Moses, Samuel, David and Elijah were figures of impressive stature in the history of Israel, but none of them could be said to be the central figure. Christians, however, were impressed that all of the loose strands of prophecy, all of the straying tendencies of history, and all of the vast hopes of Israel were summed up in God's self-disclosure in Jesus Christ. If the book of the Jews was only a collection before this time, now it became welded into a unity. The New Testament witness to the Incarnation of the Son of God *made* it one book.

A Procedure for Bible Reading

To say "Simply read it" may get at the thing we need. But there is more than one way to read the Bible. Harry Emerson Fosdick said that, as a young boy, he resolved to read the Bible all the way through, using the old method of reading three chapters a day and five chapters on Sunday. But he never succeeded in finishing because he always got stalled about halfway through Jeremiah.

Actually, this method may be the least satisfactory method of all. Reading the Bible straight through fails to take into consideration one fundamental feature of the Bible: the arrangement of the books does not correspond either to an orderly presentation of history or to a logical presentation of ideas and doctrines. Other approaches can give one an overview of the whole Bible without the tedious work of reading straight from Genesis to Revelation.

It might seem surprising, but if our aim is to get an overview, not only is it not advisable to read the Bible straight through, it is *not* advisable to read the *whole* Bible. At least that should not be our first goal.

Instead, once we recognize that the Bible is composed of

different kinds of literature, written at different times and for different purposes, we have a clue as to how one might approach getting an overview of the Bible.

A good overview will concentrate on the types of literature and the historical sections of the Bible. What I recommend is a relatively simple program of Bible study. It consists of three steps: an introductory step and two surveys of the Bible. They are rather straightforward exercises intended to give you an overall survey of Bible literature and Bible thought, as well as a survey of Bible history.

Step One: An Introduction
If I were to set out on a trip to, say, Albuquerque, New Mexico, I would first need to set firmly in my mind the location of my intended destination. I would take out a map and locate Albuquerque. Then I would find Warrensburg, Missouri, and try to determine the best route from one to the other.

I must do something like that in Bible study. Two books especially summarize the Christian idea on human nature and destiny. John's Gospel summarizes the end results of God's program of redemption, and Genesis, the present human condition. So these are the books I must read first if I am to understand from the biblical point of view where I am as well as where I am going.

Genesis, of course, is about beginnings. But it is really more than that. It is intensely a book that describes the present human condition. What we understand after reading the creation story, followed by the Fall, is the great gap between the world as it was intended and the world as it is. The first eleven chapters reveal, in an unparalleled way, the problem of our alienation from God, from creation and from one another.

The Gospel of John, on the other hand, is able to summarize the gospel message in a way that is not highly dependent on background knowledge. John not only presents some of the sayings and deeds from the story of Jesus, but he also helps us to know how to think about these things. No other book gives us more help in understanding the redemptive goal of history.

Thus we are given a view of the "end" and goal of our journey.

Step One: Read Genesis and John.

Step Two: The First Survey
The second step consists of organizing our reading of the Bible so that we get the broadest survey in the shortest period of time. The intent is to acquaint us with the variety of literature and the direction in which redemptive history takes us. In other words, our intent at this point is to become involved in the *thought* of the Bible and its *basic view of life*.

This step takes advantage of an important aspect of the make-up of Scripture. We can survey the literature of the Bible, without reading all of it, for one principal reason. Although there are sixty-six different books in the Bible, there are considerably fewer *groups* of books, from which we can select representative readings.

For example, the Old Testament canon, as it was constituted in Judaism, is composed of three classic sections; each one was a progressively later addition to the list of sacred books. The first section is the Law, or the Torah as it is called in Hebrew. The second is the Prophets. And the third is called the Writings or the Holy Writings. These three traditional divisions of the Hebrew Bible comprise *all* of the Old Testament (without, of course, the apocryphal writings). The Jews came to call their Bible the *Tanach*, which is an acronym made up of the consonants T, N and K. These are the initials for the Hebrew Law (Torah), Prophets (Nevi'im), and Writings (Ketuvim).

When the Old Testament was translated into Greek, and later into Latin, the books were rearranged to reflect a topical pattern that was also roughly chronological—although the prophets are not in chronological order. It is this arrangement that is found in our Christian Old Testament. For a comparison of the Hebrew and Christian arrangement of these books see table 1.

This second step in our first stage of Bible study, therefore,

Hebrew		Christian	
I. The Law (Torah)		**I. The Pentateuch (meaning "five scrolls")**	
Genesis	Numbers	Genesis	Numbers
Exodus	Deuteronomy	Exodus	Deuteronomy
Leviticus		Leviticus	
II. The Prophets		**II. Historical Books**	
Former prophets:		Joshua	1 & 2 Chronicles
Joshua	1 & 2 Samuel	Judges	Ezra
Judges	1 & 2 Kings	Ruth	Nehemiah
		1 & 2 Samuel	Esther
Latter prophets:		1 & 2 Kings	
Isaiah	Micah		
Jeremiah	Nahum	**III. Poetical Books**	
Ezekiel	Habakkuk	Job	Ecclesiastes
Hosea	Zephaniah	Psalms	Song of Solomon
Joel	Haggai	Proverbs	
Amos	Zechariah		
Obadiah	Malachi	**IV. Prophetical Books**	
Jonah		Isaiah	Jonah
		Jeremiah	Micah
III. The Writings		Lamentations	Nahum
Psalms	Ecclesiastes	Ezekiel	Habakkuk
Proverbs	Esther	Daniel	Zephaniah
Job	Daniel	Hosea	Haggai
Song of Solomon	Ezra	Joel	Zechariah
Ruth	Nehemiah	Amos	Malachi
Lamentations	1 & 2 Chronicles	Obadiah	

Table 1. The Hebrew Bible and Christian Old Testament

selects from each of these groups in order to gain exposure to the varieties of literature and the range of thought in the Bible. This step does not satisfy the need to gain an overview of Hebrew history. That comes later. But this is an extremely important preliminary reading. As you read the Bible—even to gain a historical perspective—the most helpful skill will be a developed sense of the purpose and tone of biblical writings. By reading the different kinds of literature and reflecting on the different purposes of these books, you will gain perspective on how to interpret them.

Not all of the biblical books can be interpreted as if they were

historical accounts, any more than they can all be
as poetical writings. By giving attention to these (
writing, you will begin to see clearly the differences ....
books like Ecclesiastes and Job, on the one hand, and the books
of Samuel and Kings, on the other.

In the New Testament is a similar, but simpler, division into
groups. There are four Gospels: Matthew, Mark, Luke and
John. There is one historical book: the Acts of the Apostles.
These are followed by epistles which include all of the rest,
though one epistle (the book of Revelation) is so entirely distinct that it belongs to a category of its own—apocalyptic.

Now, taking these general groups into consideration, we can
formulate a reading assignment to include readings from each:
Exodus will take us further into the Pentateuch and give us a
central account of Old Testament history. Ruth or Esther will
give us fascinating, narrowly focused stories out of Hebrew
history. The other historical books are reserved for our later
effort to understand the historical sequence of Israel's story.
Ecclesiastes will give us an exposure to some of the most prob-
lematic aspects of Old Testament thought. Isaiah is the first
prophet in the Old Testament canon, the most important
prophet in terms of New Testament usage, and one of the
greatest writings in the world of literature. This can be read as
among the highest expressions of prophecy. From the Gospels
we can add Matthew or Mark to the previous reading of John,
reserving Luke for the readings of historical interest. Acts and
Revelation are also set aside for later and more specialized
interest in New Testament study. The epistles can be represented by Romans.

Step Two: Read Exodus, Ruth or Esther, Ecclesiastes, Isaiah,
Matthew or Mark, and Romans.

Step Three: The Second Survey
Without historical sequence, our Bible study lacks a vitally necessary framework. As we have already seen, the religion of the

Bible is inextricably tied to history, and without an understanding of the sequential events of history, we do not really have an adequate view of biblical thought.

Now, therefore, we want to organize our reading to include those books that unfold for us the history of Israel, the life of Christ and the story of the early church.

Part of the work has already been done, since in our first two steps we read Genesis and Exodus. These two books introduce the history of Israel from its patriarchal beginnings (Abraham, Isaac, Jacob and his sons) to the great exodus from slavery in Egypt and until the tribes of Israel encamp at Sinai.

We can now take up the history of Israel in the wilderness, before entering the Promised Land, by reading Numbers. This book leads us from the departure from Sinai through the wilderness wanderings and up to the time the people of Israel stood poised on the eastern shores of the Jordan river, ready to enter Canaan.

Joshua takes us through the Canaan conquest. Judges deals with the more than two centuries of tribal confederacy which existed after the time of Joshua and before the days of the monarchy. Afterward, we can trace the history of the kingdoms of Israel from their inception under the prophetic leadership of Samuel, through the glorious days of David and Solomon, through the successive crises of division, the Assyrian aggression and the Babylonian deportation. This central sweep of kingdom history is treated most extensively in the two books of Samuel and the two books of Kings.

In 1 and 2 Chronicles we find a recapitulation of history from Genesis to the Babylonian exile and the destruction of the temple, focusing primarily on the time from David's reign on. This gives the reader a new view of the same history with a further interpretation of the lessons of history.

Finally, Ezra and Nehemiah begin where the Chronicles end (and also where 2 Kings left us) and give an account of the return from exile and the reconstruction of the nation.

These books should be read in order. Read not to absorb the minutiae of Israel's history but to gain a solid command of its broad sweep. One way to relate the smaller incidents to the larger context of history is to read this history with a simple chronological chart alongside (see table 2). As you use this chart, or any chart on Old Testament history, keep in mind that the more remote the date in history, the more likely the dates are to be imprecise.

Surveying history in the New Testament is simpler. But we must remember that the world of the New Testament is considerably removed from that of the Old Testament. Jesus and Ezra are as far removed from each other as we are from William Shakespeare and Francis Bacon. Much had happened to the world and to Palestine during the intervening years.

New Testament history is easier for us for two reasons. First, it was a history acted out under the influence of the Greek and Roman world, and these Western cultures are much more familiar to us than those great powers of the East that exerted their influence over Old Testament days: Assyria, Babylon and Persia. We are much more at home with Tiberius Caesar than we are with Tiglath-Pileser III. We are reasonably familiar with the Mediterranean regions of Italy, Greece, Spain and the provinces of Asia Minor (parts of modern Turkey), all of which play major or minor roles in New Testament history. But once we move east beyond the Jordan river—into Syria and Persia—our geographical orientation is less sure.

The second reason New Testament history is easier is simply that Old Testament history covers at least a millennium and a half (without the early history of Genesis 1-11), while the New Testament covers less than a century. For anyone, East or West, it is easier to command a knowledge of the brief New Testament period than the generations upon generations of the Old Testament people who often went through kaleidescopic changes in historical and political circumstances.

For a brief survey of New Testament history it is necessary to read only two books—Luke and Acts—written by the same author as two parts of a single historical writing. Both were written by Luke the physician, a gentile friend and companion of Paul's, who endeavored to "write an orderly account" of those early events in the history of the church.

Step Three: Read Numbers, Joshua, Judges, 1 and 2 Samuel, 1 and 2 Kings, 1 and 2 Chronicles, Ezra, Nehemiah, Luke and Acts.

1. **Primeval history (undated)**   Genesis 1—11
   Adam and Eve
   Cain and Abel
   Cain's line   Seth's line
   Noah
   Ham, Shem and Japheth (division by nations)
   The Tower of Babel (division by languages)

2. **The Patriarchal Period (ca 1900-1700 B.C.)**   Genesis 12—50
   Abram (Abraham)
   Isaac
   Jacob (Israel)
   The Sons of Israel (focus on Joseph)
   Settlement in Egypt

3. **Israel in Egypt (ca 1690-1300)**
   Hyksos rule in Egypt (1710-1570)
   The "New Kingdom" (1570-1200)
   The 19th dynasty and the great delta building
   program of Seti I and Ramses II (ca 1303-1200)

4. **Exodus and the Wilderness Wanderings**   Exodus
   (ca 1300 to the time of the Conquest)   Numbers
   Moses   Deuteronomy
   Kadesh-Barnea   Joshua
   40 years of the exodus generation
   Joshua

5. **The Tribal Confederacy (ca 1250-1020)**   Judges
   Period of Judges   Ruth

6. **The United Monarchy (ca 1020-922)**   1 & 2 Samuel
   Saul (1020-1000)   1 & 2 Kings
   David (1000-961)   1 & 2 Chronicles
   Solomon (961-922)

Table 2. An Outline of Old Testament History (continued on p. 69)

7. The Divided Monarchy: Judah and Israel
A. Judah—the Southern Kingdom (922-587)
    The Davidic Dynasty (one dynasty, twenty kings)
B. Israel—the Northern Kingdom (922-722)
    (nine dynasties, nineteen kings)

8. Exile
Samaria falls to Assyria (722)
Jerusalem falls to Nebuchadnezzar II (587)

9. The Return   Esther
Cyrus, king of Persia, takes Babylon (539-538)   Ezra
First exiles return with Zerubbabel (537)   Nehemiah
The Temple is rebuilt and dedicated (516)
The return under the leadership of Nehemiah (464-423)
The return led by Ezra (404)
The close of the Old Testament record (ca 400)

Table 2. An Outline of Old Testament History

Using the Whole-Book Method

By now you should see that this is a way to survey the essential parts of the Bible's history and literature without the tedium of reading straight through. After completing these three steps you will have read twenty-one books rather than the entire sixty-six; yet you will have become familiar with every large section of Bible literature and have surveyed the history of the Bible people. If you were using my Revised Standard Version of the Bible (Oxford Annotated Edition), that would mean that instead of plowing through 1,514 pages of text, you would have done a substantial reading of the whole Bible in about 777 pages. That is still a considerable amount of reading. But once we have cut the task literally in half, the work of surveying the whole Bible no longer seems as formidable as it might have.

A few practical suggestions now about how to put this survey to its best use. None of these should complicate the job of thoughtful reading; in fact they should help you to focus on the Bible itself.

1. *Keep a notebook.* Taking notes on what you read helps focus your mind and enforces attentiveness. The notes should be

meaningful to you when they are reread, but they need not be highly structured. The last thing you want to do is get caught up in making a formal outline of your reading with careful notations of sections and subsections. Instead make a free, informal outline, noting where each new topic begins.

For instance, if you are reading Genesis, you might note the beginning of the Abraham story by writing, "Terah, Abram's father, moves family from Ur to Haran—11:26ff." Then note anything of interest you find in that section. Use your own symbols or abbreviations to recall passages that you want to reread or memorize. Also use this same notebook format to record your reaction to the passages you read. What were you thinking when you read this passage? What images and ideas did it evoke for you? What questions came to mind?

At the end of a book, pause and reflect on what was the whole effect of the book. What major ideas, events or emotions are evident in this writing? Write a paragraph or two to describe your immediate reaction to the book after having read it. Later you will likely find that quite a number of other thoughts come to the surface that were generated by this earlier reading; in fact, the later, more developed thinking on the subject may be much more fruitful than your more immediate impressions. Nevertheless, this is an important step for the simple reason that it helps to get that process of reflection started. Many of your better ideas, developed at a subliminal level, may begin with consciously stirring up your first impressions right after completing the reading of a book or a large section.

2. *Accompany all Bible reading with prayer.* The Bible is a volume that yields to prayer and nothing short of earnest, continual prayer. Emil Brunner said that all good theology begins and ends in prayer. The same is true of studying Scripture.

If you believe, as I do, that the Holy Spirit inspired these writings and that the first thing about the writings—what lay behind them all—is an experience of God, then unless we can refer to that primary experience in our own lives we will not understand the experience of those who wrote in the white heat of an encounter with the living God.

I would not want to suggest a formal pattern of prayer and study, but I think there should be some kind of pattern, one which you have found helpful and personally rewarding. Try to develop a rhythm of study and prayer—one reinforcing the other. Prayer should lead to a hunger for study and a readiness to absorb more of the written word; study should prepare us for prayer, leading us to desire the experience of which these pages continually speak. I cannot imagine what attraction a cold, lifeless, academic study of Scripture would have. To know Paul truly—to understand his writings in any meaningful sense—is to identify with the passionate devotion of Paul to a living, present Savior.

The genuine study of any subject cannot be only a distant, purely objective examination. The best scientists, the best mathematicians, the greatest Shakespearean scholars all have submerged their whole selves into the study of their disciplines. Mentally and emotionally, they are absorbed in their subject, making it yield to the full force of their mind, sentiment and will. No less is necessary for Bible study. And, to my mind, no door but prayer admits us to the world the people of the Bible know. Not technique or educational background, not even a visit to the Holy Land, opens the world of the Bible to us. All of these things can help us, but only by prayer can we gain entrance.

3. *Do some parallel reading in modern reference works.* At this stage you will want to be careful not to get sidetracked and end up reading things about the Bible instead of reading the Bible itself. Put off reading the heavier and more extensive works until later in your program of study. (I will suggest some general readings in the next few chapters.) Now is an excellent time to read reference articles on broad topics from Bible dictionaries and encyclopedias. At the end of this chapter is a list of some of the more valuable reference works.

For a few examples, you might look up articles (and take detailed notes) on "Old Testament Canon," "New Testament Canon," "Israel," "Jesus Christ," "The Kingdom of God,"

"Monotheism," "The Holy Spirit," or any number of others that might help you to orient your thinking on topics you encounter while reading.

4. *Set definite times for personal Bible study.* Two words of caution. First, do not confuse this time of study with your regular devotional period. This regular reading of Scripture is not a substitute for prayer and meditation. Second, although regular times of study should be observed and become a part of one's personal discipline, they need not be *daily* periods of study. Many people may find that a three-hour stretch of reading, perhaps on Saturday morning, is more productive than thirty minutes a day for six days.

Decide first how many hours a week you can realistically expect to devote to Bible study. For some it may be no more than an hour or so; for others it may be more. After that, you do not always need to schedule evenly divided periods of time. You might schedule thirty minutes on Monday evening, an hour on Tuesday, another thirty-minute session during Wednesday's lunch break. Then, since Thursday through Saturday are heavily scheduled, you might plan to avoid committing these days.

Whatever schedule you decide on, the point is to determine to meet it each week. You might also schedule certain hours during one day (Sunday perhaps) that would serve as a make-up time for unscheduled interruptions during the week.

5. *Be persistent.* Next to prayer this is the most important of all. The Bible is not always easy reading. Sometimes it is, but often it requires the pressure of a determined will before it gives up the secrets that have made it a book to endure the ages.

The good news in all of this is that reading the Bible does not require—as some would likely think—raw courage to overcome a dreadfully dull task. People who have actually read the Bible extensively agree that no other book invites persistence and excites the active mind as much as the Bible does. Speaking of the Gospel of Matthew, Robert Louis Stevenson wrote, "I believe it would startle and move anyone, if he could make a certain effort of imagination, and read it freshly like a book, not droningly and dull like a portion of the Bible."

Great writers, who know how to hold the attention of a reading public, witness to the drawing power of the Bible by the many ways the Bible shapes and influences their writing. George Eckman wrote:

We are not aware how extensive is the influence of the Bible upon our foremost writers until we have carefully pondered the works of such poets as Spenser, Shakespeare, Chilton, Pope, Scott, Cowper, Wordsworth, Tennyson, Young, the Brownings, Longfellow and others and of such prose writers as Bacon, Addison, Johnson, Macaulay, Carlyle, Irving, Ruskin, Lowell, and many more. Spenser, we are told, studied the prophetic writings before he wrote his Faerie Queene. Lord Bacon has seventy allusions to the Scriptures in twenty-four of his essays. In Bishop Charles Wordsworth's book on Shakespeare's Knowledge and Use of the Bible allusions or quotations in thirty-seven plays are indicated, a fact of great significance when it is remembered that Shakespeare died only four years after the King James Version was published in full. There are more than one hundred allusions to the Bible in Mrs. Browning's Aurora Leigh. A careful study of Tennyson has asserted that there are nearly three hundred direct references to the Bible in his poems. By actual count upward of three hundred and thirty references to the Bible have been found in works of Longfellow. . . . Ruskin [said] that to the discipline of his early years in the Bible he owes "the best part of my taste in literature, and, once knowing the Bible it was not possible for me to write superficial and formal English."[3]

Eckman wrote this passage in 1915. Had he been writing today, he would doubtless have mentioned T. S. Eliot, Joseph Conrad, G. K. Chesterton, Sherwood Anderson, Thomas Wolfe, William Faulkner, Charles Williams, C. S. Lewis, J. R. R. Tolkein, Dorothy Sayers, Walker Percy, Robert Penn Warren, Allen Tate, George Santayana and others. He might have mentioned that a poet and critic like John Crowe Ransom was convinced by his reading of the Bible that modern thought and literature needed to be infused with more of the spirit of Old Testament theology.[4] Or he might have said that T. S. Eliot thought it was the Christian reader's responsibility to "scrutinize their reading, especially of works of imagination, with explicit ethical and theological standards"[5]—which they gain, of course, from the great texts of their faith.

If such testimony as this exists among those who know how to command a reading audience, those who know the art of telling stories, engaging thought, evoking mental images, then can we imagine that the Bible itself is less attractive to even the less discriminating reader? If thirst is gratified by the streams running down the mountainside, will it not revel in the discovery of that hidden spring from which those streams flow? It is not the least of blessings that the very reading that many people think of as reading for "improvement," once discovered, is also a source of great joy.

General Reference Works for Introductory Reading

The Interpreter's Dictionary of the Bible. Ed. George Buttrick. Nashville: Abingdon, 1962.

Harper's Encyclopedia of Bible Life. Madeleine S. and J. Lane Miller. New York: Harper and Row, 1978.

The New Bible Dictionary. Ed. J. D. Douglas. Grand Rapids: Eerdmans, 1975.

The Biblical World: A Dictionary of Biblical Archaeology. Ed. Charles F. Pfeiffer. Nashville: Broadman, 1976.

5
How to
Read the
New Testament

You might be surprised that I turn next to the New Testament in thinking about Bible study. The Old Testament, after all, is the older and larger part of the canon of Scripture. The New Testament often quotes the Old Testament; its view of the world is fed by the Old Testament; and the early church had one collection of writings that they esteemed above all others—again what we call the Old Testament. So, why begin with the New Testament before mastering the Old?

Before we look at reasons, it is good to remind ourselves of the importance of the Old Testament. A highly regarded New Testament scholar wrote that "of all the 'helps' which assist the reader to understand the New Testament, the Old Testament is by far the most important."[1] It is the fountainhead of the New Testament understanding of God in Christ. Jesus' own attitude toward the law should govern a Christian's regard for the Old Covenant: the new has come in order to fulfill the old—not to replace it.

After a survey of both Old and New Testaments, however, a concentrated look at the New Testament is well worthwhile. A long-time teacher of biblical studies at a state university told me

that he used to recommend that, if students could not take both
Old Testament and New Testament surveys, they should take
New Testament alone. Why? Because when you study the New
Testament, he said, you are at least exposed to some of both
testaments. I thought that was an interesting comment from a
man who cared a great deal about students learning the Bible.
He recognized that the New Testament never stands by itself—
it is not simply additional Scripture. Instead, it is a way of viewing the Old Testament in the light of an overpowering new
work of God.

The earliest Christians—most of them Jews who grew up with
the Hebrew Bible, the Septuagint translation or the Targums in
Aramaic—lived in an atmosphere charged with excitement
over seeing the Scripture take on new life. Imagine a first-
century Jew reading Psalm 22 in light of the recent events of
the death and resurrection of Jesus.

> My God, my God, why hast thou forsaken me?
> Why art thou so far from helping me, from the
>   words of my groaning? . . .
>
> I am poured out like water,
>   and all my bones are out of joint;
> My heart is like wax,
>   it is melted within my breast; . . .
>   thou dost lay me in the dust of death.
>
> Yea, dogs are round about me;
>   a company of evildoers encircle me;
>   they have pierced my hands and feet—
> I can count all my bones—
>   they stare and gloat over me;
> they divide my garments among them,
>   and for my raiment they cast lots. (Ps 22:1, 14-18)

As the psalm was written, and as it was read for many centuries,
it was not considered a messianic poem at all. It was a lament

of David who was mortally ill. The comments made in the notes
of the Oxford Revised Standard Version are quite appropriate:

> The psalmist's misery is aggravated by the mockery of those
> who regard his illness as proof that God has forsaken him.
> . . . His detractors behave like savage animals. . . . He is so
> nearly dead that his neighbors and relatives have already
> begun to divide his property.[2]

But isn't it obvious why the early Christians were so amazed
with the way this psalm—which was quoted by Jesus on the
cross—corresponded with the details of Jesus' crucifixion? Of
course, the psalm is about the ailing David. But at the same time
here were new events that brought the old psalm alive and
charged it with new meaning and new associations.

In other words, the Old Testament had not only a concrete,
historical meaning, but it also was capable of giving birth to
new meanings. It described the way God works among us. And
now these early believers had seen him act in just that way
again. In fact, so concentrated were his recent acts in the person of Jesus Christ, that all of those ancient events were supported, fulfilled and given even greater content than before.
Bishop Stephen Neill once wrote that "in Jesus Christ a force
of inestimable magnitude began to operate within the world of
men."[3] And in a wonderfully eloquent passage he goes on to
show how this great force began to work a change in the future
of the world. Yet that "force of inestimable magnitude" also
worked backwards and transformed men's view of the history
they had already experienced. It was not changed utterly; the
Jews who were followers of Christ and the Jews who were not
followers still shared the same religious view of the world. But
now, because of Christ, there was a new accent, a new hope that
emerged from the older prophecies, and a new recognition of
the living power of God. Followers of Christ were reading the
Old Testament now in the light of New Testament experiences.

My point is that to some degree we need to do the same. That
is why, at this stage, New Testament study precedes Old Testament.

First, however, let's anticipate an objection. There will be those who imagine that this means we are simply reinterpreting the Old Testament from a particular ideological point of view. And rather than reading the Old Testament for what it really says, or what it was intended to say, we simply read it out of a determined Christian bias. It is always possible to do that and to read the Old Testament carelessly as if we were only mining it for things that support what we already believe. But there is something more to discovering truth in this way than entertaining a bias, and it often happens to work "backwards" on events the same way we read the Old Testament in light of the New.

I studied for several years under the direction of the well-known theologian Dale Moody. Before I had ever met him, I had read some of his works. I could certainly understand what was being said in those works, and I could imagine what the author looked like—although that was of no great importance in reading his theology. But after I came to know him personally a peculiar thing happened when I read his writing. As I read the words, I had a sense of how he would speak them. I would recognize pet topics, little twists of irony; I could see the great enthusiasm and vigor with which he launched into certain arguments. And along with his nailing down a favorite point, I could see his knowing wink to a student in the front row, and with each firm warning I could imagine his characteristic wagging of a finger in the air.

Now, the question is: Have these subsequent experiences—which now influence my reading of Moody—made my understanding less reliable? Certainly not. It has given me a point of view that I did not have before. While my reading is no longer that of a neutral and objective critic, nevertheless, the later experiences of Moody-in-the-flesh have made my readings of Moody-in-print more incisive and reliable than ever before.

In the same way, we can say that there comes a time in the study of the Bible when the New Testament should be given a more thorough survey. And that time properly comes *before*, not after, the Old Testament is given a similar reading. Such a reading gives us a definite point of view from which we will later understand and interpret the Old Testament.

Preparation for New Testament Study

Though the study of individual books, which we will take up in chapter seven, is the real heart of Bible study, such study will be much more meaningful if we give attention to two aspects in a survey of the New Testament. The first aspect is that of the arrangement of the New Testament books. And the second aspect is the relationship of books within the various categories of writings in the New Testament.

The Arrangement of New Testament Books

I have an anthology on my desk made up of essays and articles from a variety of authors on general biblical themes. Now the editor had some purpose in mind, I am sure, when he began to arrange these articles in their present order. But the truth is that it would make little difference if the articles were shuffled around and appeared in an entirely different order. A reader can read one article and then never look at the book again and still profit just as well from that one article.

Now, even to someone who is casually acquainted with the New Testament, it ought to be clear that these writings are not so constituted. There is, in fact, a pattern in the arrangement. And, furthermore, the arrangement itself tells us some significant things about the books themselves.

We have already seen that the twenty-seven books of the New Testament are made up of four Gospels, one historical account of the early church, twenty-one letters, and one apocalyptic writing. All of these writings are headed by a Gospel—placed immediately after the Old Testament—which is the most Hebrew and most closely tied to the Old Testament of all the New Testament writings: the Gospel of Matthew. Above all of the others, it looks back to the Old Testament as its source of reference. Each incident in the life of Christ is related to prophecies from the old texts. Any Bible that clearly marks quotations from the Old Testament will reveal that Matthew—more than the others—is filled with references to the prophecies concerning Christ. The most characteristic phrase for Matthew, not surprisingly, is "that it might be fulfilled." Only a brief glance

at the first few chapters of Matthew will show how wonderfully dependent Matthew is upon the Old Testament Scriptures.

Then at the end of these twenty-seven books is the strange
and wonderful book of Revelation. It is a letter, a prophecy,
and—most of all—an apocalypse. Its very title ("Apocalypse"
from the Greek, or "Revelation" coming from the Latin) means
an "unveiling," referring to a drawing back of the curtain on
the mysteries of the future which includes God's final redemptive acts. While the first book looks back on the history of God's
elect people, their national history, and their hopes from the
narrow perspective of events at one end of the Mediterranean
world, the last book opens up on a vast and universal conclusion that is to be fulfilled in the future. The whole of the New
Testament moves from promise to hope, from national messiah
to universal savior. Both of these perspectives are necessary
and complementary; and Matthew, with its look to the past,
together with Revelation, with its view of the future, symbolize
and summarize the whole of New Testament concerns.

The Gospels
Now let us look at some of the different kinds of writing in the
New Testament. The first thing that confronts us in the list of
New Testament books is that we have not one harmonized Gospel on the ministry of Christ, but four somewhat distinct Gospels. Why four? Why were not all of the pertinent facts drawn
together to constitute one authoritative book on the words and
works of Jesus Christ? What is the meaning of this fourfold
presentation of the life of Christ?

The opportunity to harmonize the Gospel accounts did not
escape the attention of the earliest church. Before the end of
the second century, a Syrian Christian named Tatian labored
to produce a unified Gospel account that became known as the
Diatessaron. The effort was impressive enough that some parts
of the early church began to consider the work canonical. But
the church later officially rejected the *Diatessaron* and maintained the four separate accounts—our only really direct wit-

nesses to the earthly life of our Lord.

One way to read these Gospels with better understanding is to look at the significance of the effort to preserve all four of these Gospel accounts without confusing or intermingling their stories. In the early church, and even today, the Gospels were represented by four symbolic creatures: a lion, an ox or calf, a man and an eagle. These symbolic creatures are found first in the book of Ezekiel, in the first great theophany that the prophet experienced while in exile (Ezek 1:10). Some commentators have taken these to represent the four classes of creatures: man to represent humankind, the lion to represent the highest of wild beasts, the ox to represent the highest of domestic animals, and the eagle to represent the noblest of birds.

Men of great insight into personality, however, from William Blake to C. G. Jung, have seen these symbols as representing aspects of the whole personality: intelligence, emotion, intuition and sensation.

However we see these, we would not be incorrect in saying that they signify four aspects of God's own self-disclosure— whether intrinsically in his personality, or extrinsically in his created order. These four symbols are associated with God because they reveal something of God himself. In the Revelation they appear again (Rev 4:6-7), and in this connection Augustine gives us the most helpful insights into the use of these symbols.

Let me summarize and expand a bit on what Augustine has to say about these four symbols. Then we can see that these are four ways that God is revealed in Christ.[4]

The lion represents kingship and is related to the Gospel of Matthew. Remember that in Matthew Jesus' claim to the Davidic throne and his fulfillment of the Davidic prophecies are most fully emphasized. There the preaching on the kingdom of heaven is most fully preserved; no other gospel mentions that kingdom so prominently. The genealogy of Jesus at the very beginning of the Gospel concentrates on David in order to show the legitimacy of Jesus' claim to the title of king, and it extends to Abraham to emphasize that this messiah-king belongs to the pure stock of Abraham. He is of no proselyte line. Further, it is in Matthew that the magi come from the east inquiring after the newborn king.

The man symbol is related to Mark. Mark has no genealogy to trace the kingly or priestly pedigree of Jesus. Rather, his emphasis is on Jesus as man, without the official claims that go beyond simple humanity. Furthermore, the strongest theological theme in Mark is that Jesus Christ is shown to be the Son of God—and he is revealed as such by virtue of his perfect humanity. Because Jesus is obedient—as man was intended to be obedient—he fulfilled the intended role of humankind. But paradoxically, the fact that he does so—that fact that he discloses *true* humanity, rather than fallen humanity—is witness to the truth that he is the Son of God.

The ox or calf symbolizes Luke. The calf was the pre-eminent sacrifice administered by the priest. So the calf signifies the priestly office of Christ, and that office figures prominently in the Lukan account. The priest's function is to represent man before God. He is, first of all, a *man* who stands in the breach between God and man in order to make expiation for sins and to renew our access to God. Thus Luke's genealogy traces Jesus' lineage all the way back to Adam. Augustine points out that Luke's Gospel begins with Zechariah the priest and the relation of that family to Jesus through Zechariah's wife Elizabeth, who was herself a descendant of Aaron, the first high priest. Luke, more than the others, prolongs and emphasizes that last journey to Jerusalem where Jesus offered the superior sacrifice at the holy city of the priestly cult. Not only that, but like the high priest entering the holy of holies on the day of Atonement, he faced the altar of atonement sacrifice utterly alone.

Finally, the Gospel of John—that great essay on the divine nature of Christ—is symbolized by the lofty figure of the eagle. The eagle flies alone, high above the landscape, with the power of vision to spot its prey from great distances and to swoop down unerringly to execute its mission. This lone, transcendent figure signifies the omnipresent Godhead. In John we find the divinity of Christ most clearly and most eloquently pronounced.

The origin of Christ is not revealed in a genealogy, but in an opening paragraph on the creative and redemptive eternal "logos" or "Word" of God. John is, furthermore, not as concerned as the rest with reporting the outward events of Jesus' life so much as revealing the inner meaning of these events. While Matthew, Mark and Luke concentrate on the shape and substance of Jesus' earthly life, John focuses on its significance. In John we find the great passages, such as John 3:16—"For God so loved the world that he gave his only Son, that whoever believes in him . . ."—which, while not direct teachings of Jesus, nevertheless tell us the significance of his life.

That point leads us to another important observation about the Gospels. The most significant distinction among the Gospel accounts is that which divides John, this highly theological and interpretive Gospel, from the other three. Matthew, Mark and Luke are so much alike—their material so precisely the same in many instances—that they are known as the "synoptic" Gospels. *Synoptic* means simply "to see together." When they are compared it becomes obvious that almost all of the verses in Mark are reproduced by either Matthew or Luke. And, furthermore, great blocks of sayings from Jesus appear both in Matthew and Luke that do not appear in Mark.

This is not the place to discuss the explanations for these similarities. But it is important to see that these three—probably relying on a common source as well as on each other—are remarkably similar. John, on the other hand, is quite different in wording, style and point of view.

Any reader of the Gospels will be helped by noting that while the synoptics deal with particulars in the life of Christ, John emphasizes the general. The synoptics focus on the humanity of Christ in order to disclose his divinity; John, on the other hand, assumes his divinity and shows the significance of his humanity. The synoptics report the public discourses of Christ, while John concentrates on the private teachings. The synoptics emphasize the parables of Jesus, while John emphasizes the direct and didactic teachings of our Lord. The synoptics focus on the Galilean ministry of Jesus, while John focuses on the

Judean ministry. The synoptics and John do not force us to choose one or the other, as if they stood in contradiction to each other; instead they complement and support their mutual testimony. Both are needed.

Acts

The book of Acts stands in a peculiar double relationship to the other New Testament writings. It is, in a sense, a part of the synoptic writings, since it is the second part of a two-part work by Luke. Sometimes the Gospel and Acts are referred to as the single writing of Luke-Acts, because their continuity and their common theme, as well as their common authorship, are evident. In the introduction to Acts, Luke refers back to his "first book" and addresses himself to Theophilus, just as he had done in the Gospel.

Additionally, however, the Acts of the Apostles serves as a vital link between the Gospels in the first part of the New Testament and the Epistles in the latter part. Luke points toward the gentile mission, which becomes a reality in Acts. Luke tells of the messianic person; Acts tells of the messianic people. Luke sees the cross and resurrection as the goal of the gospel story; Acts has the cross and resurrection as background. Luke concerns the promise of the Spirit; Acts, the presence and power of the Spirit. So, in every way, Acts leads beyond the Gospels and gives us a historical opening into the world that would now receive the Christian gospel. And it was to that world—the world of the Romans and the Corinthians and the Ephesians—that the Epistles of the New Testament were first addressed.

Acts gives us a link between Palestine, that peculiar environment in which monotheism was born and developed, and the outside pagan world that would in one short century be transformed by a religion that worshiped the God of Israel. It tells us how a world divided among gods and nations of people—which was temporarily united by the iron law of Rome—became the closest thing to a world brotherhood that this planet has ever known. Bishop Stephen Neill says, "Even a casual reader is likely to feel as he passes to Luke and Acts that he has left one world and passed into another."[5] It *was* another world, because already Luke was giving witness to the mystery of a transformation unlike any the world has ever seen. It is no wonder, then, that "in many ways," as Donald Guthrie wrote, "the Epistles are not fully intelligible until they are read against the background of the book of Acts."[6]

The Epistles

Nothing tells us more about the nature of the New Testament writings than the fact that most of the writings are correspondence. Some have tried to make much of the fine distinction between an "epistle" and a "letter." But either of these terms will convey what is centrally important about the New Testament writings from Romans to Jude; namely, that they are written in response to specific circumstances of the day, often with particular people in mind, and more than occasionally as one side of a series of correspondence between two writers.

This fact led William Barclay to comment that the disadvantage in having these letters is that it is a little like listening in on one side of a telephone conversation. You know what is being said on this side, but you can only guess what is being said by the other party. In 2 Thessalonians, for instance, Paul alludes to some things he had said during his visit to Thessalonica about the one who would restrain the "man of perdition." So he simply says, in effect, "you already know to whom I am referring" (see 2 Thess 2:5-6). *They* may have known, since they were there when he spoke to them, but we don't! And, of course, the passage has been the subject of considerable speculation on the matter.

If that is a disadvantage, however, the advantages—as Barclay would readily agree—are enormously greater. The fact that it is correspondence—with all of its uncertain allusions, and with all of its happenstance concerns (like Paul asking Timothy to bring him his cloak from Troas in 2 Timothy 4)—means that we learn about the gospel on the basis of the most personal of all forms of literature. The question must be posed, then, "Could we really learn these things in any better way?" How

much could a doctrinal essay improve on Paul's sensitive letter
to his friend Philemon on behalf of his new convert—and
Philemon's runaway slave—Onesimus?

In these letters we do not read of teachings from a detached
and objective point of view; instead they are undergirded by the
passions and sentiments called forth by circumstances. Philippians we can understand not only by what it says, but by the
reflected feeling of gratitude and anticipation that shows forth
from every paragraph. In Galatians we do not have cool analysis, but an argument strengthened and driven by righteous
anger and steely conviction.

Letters, in other words, convey to us more than mental processes; they convey the whole man: his sentiment, his intellect,
his passion and his hope. As Michael Polanyi and others have
shown, religious knowledge is conveyed significantly through
every level of human awareness. The rational understanding is
important—and it is the major component of the epistolary
form—but we also *know* things at a tacit and subrational level.
Nothing conveys these deeper levels of personal experience
and knowledge better than written correspondence that comes
out of life's circumstances.

The Pauline Epistles

The letters or epistles are made up of two main groups: those
that are written by Paul and those that belong to several other
writers. Of the thirteen letters that are from Paul, nine are
addressed to churches and four to individuals (see table 3).

Church Letters		Pastoral Letters
Romans	Philippians	1 Timothy
1 Corinthians	Colossians	2 Timothy
2 Corinthians	1 Thessalonians	Titus
Galatians	2 Thessalonians	Philemon*
Ephesians		

Table 3. The Pauline Letters

*Many students of the New Testament do not include Philemon in the category known as the "pastoral epistles"
and allow it to stand alone. However, I believe there are strong reasons for including it as a pastoral letter, not
the least of which is that it reflects a distinctly pastoral concern of Paul for Onesimus, for Philemon and for the
church at Colossae.

Some scholars note that the arrangement of the nine church letters seems to follow a pattern of beginning with the longest letter and ending with the shortest. There are, however, other interesting matters to be observed.

For instance, the church letters seem to be grouped around three general themes. The theme that dominates Romans through Galatians is the question of justification: How does one become right before God? The second theme, found significantly in Ephesians through Philippians is that of sanctification: How does one become holy before God? And the third theme, glorification, is the principal concern of 1 and 2 Thessalonians. The question here is: What can we hope for from God?

One group looks toward the *past* in the justifying work of Christ on the cross. One emphasizes the *present*, as Christ is revealed in his church. The third looks toward the *future* in Christ's promise of his coming. None of these statements can be taken categorically, of course, since they *all* speak of justification, sanctification and glorification. But nevertheless the letters do tend to be preoccupied in turn with (1) the cross (Romans through Galatians), (2) the church (Ephesians, Philippians and Colossians) and (3) the Second Coming (1 and 2 Thessalonians).

The other four letters—1 and 2 Timothy, Titus, and Philemon—obviously belong to a different category.[7] They are written to individuals rather than to churches. Timothy was a Greek convert to the Christian faith, a noted protégé of Paul who is mentioned also in the book of Acts. Titus is also a younger Christian for whom Paul was mentor and counselor. He is mentioned prominently in Paul's letters, although he is not mentioned in Acts. Some have speculated that he was Luke's brother.

Philemon brings to our attention another intriguing pattern in the letters of Paul. For a long time people have found it difficult to categorize. What is the book about? Why is this book included in the canon?

Its subject matter seems so bound to Paul's concern about one runaway slave and his owner. There are no broad and timeless teachings on sin, salvation, or human nature and des-

tiny. Romans and Galatians—though they are addressed to concrete circumstances—have general principles as their topic of
concern. Philemon does not. It is about Paul, Philemon and
Onesimus.

Paul's letters thus run from the broadest, most general and
most universal teachings all the way to the narrowest, most
particular applications. Romans was written to a church Paul
had never visited, about principles held in common with all
Christians. Philemon was written to a particular man that Paul
knew well enough to predict his response to an urgent appeal.

Romans is the most universal of Paul's letters. It speaks not
only of all Christians, but of all people. *All* is the thematic word.
"The wrath of God is revealed . . . against *all* ungodliness and
wickedness" (Rom 1:18). "Since *all* have sinned . . ." (Rom
3:23). "Then as one man's trespass led to condemnation for *all*
men, so one man's act of righteousness leads to acquittal and
life for *all* men" (Rom 5:18).

Philemon, by contrast, is so particular that one has trouble
abstracting any general lesson at all. The letter is not clearly
about justification, or grace, or faith, or love. In a sense it is
about all of these and a few more pertinent topics as well. But
the real point is that the letter is about Philemon, Onesimus
and Paul. Here we don't have general principles *explained;* instead we have general principles *worked out* in real life.

Therefore, the letters of Paul, read attentively, lead from the
broadest consideration to the narrowest point possible: the
heart of the individual. And they lead from the most theoretical
of considerations to the most practical: the relationship of one
person to another. Throughout the letters we have the human
soul laid bare and the heart of God revealed on a multiplicity
of levels. Here love is enjoined in principle; there it shows
through in Paul's concern for a messenger boy. Here the gospel
is said to be a power; there it rescues an endangered runaway
slave. Here Christ is said to be the one to whom every knee
shall bow; there Paul prostrates himself before the all-conquer-
ing majesty of Christ. The lesson of Christianity is made abstract enough to be applied everywhere, to everyone and in

every situation; and it is made concrete enough to be proven practical in the lives of real people.

The General Epistles

No one is altogether sure why these letters were called the general or catholic epistles. Some have held that while the church first recognized the authority of Paul's letters, they later included these others from James, John, Peter and Jude, which come from a more general group of authors. Others believe that the content of the letters, covering a broad scope of church doctrine, would properly be designated "catholic" or "general" and they were thus given this name by the church. Still others contend that, while some letters were considered canonical by the Eastern church and others by the Western church, these few were universally recognized with only a minimum of objection to their authority. Others simply point to the fact that, while Paul's letters were addressed to specific local churches or individuals, these are destined for the whole wide world of the church. And the only objection to this last opinion is that 2 and 3 John are apparently addressed to individuals.

Whatever may be the real and original purpose of this designation, we can be sure that all of the explanations are a clue to something important about the letters themselves. There are, of course, seven of these letters: James, 1 Peter, 2 Peter, 1 John, 2 John, 3 John and Jude. They are traditionally ascribed to four figures intimately related to Jesus in his earthly life. Peter and John were two of his chief apostles. James and Jude were his brothers. The authorship of these letters is far from a settled affair among scholars. Nor has there ever been a time when agreement on who wrote the letters was complete. However this may be, the traditional view of the letters' authors bears a clear message: Christianity is more than a system of thought; it is more than a way of life; it is, in a most comprehensive way, a witness to Jesus Christ. James may speak of how a Christian ought to live, and John of how a Christian ought to think, but both of these derive their authority from their relationship to their one Lord.

In speaking to the whole of the church throughout the world, these letters show how Christianity breaks out of the mold of religions that rely on local attachments and national identities. The one gospel finds its source in the one God; it is revealed in the one Savior and delivered to one world. Distinctions remain, but divisions are brought to an end. Since all believers become one in Jesus Christ, they can be addressed as a body who have more in common to unite them than they have distinctions to separate them. The letters can be general or catholic because they are addressed to a world that has overcome barriers in a common brotherhood.

But more than all of these, the general epistles address essentials in the life and thought of Christian people. James addresses the subject of good works. Peter holds out the virtue of hope. John is the apostle of love. And Jude is the one who contends for an undefiled faith. Here is the full scope of the products of a Christian life: faith, hope and love—all of which issue in works that do glory to God.

All of these letters can be read in the space of an hour or so. But with these brief letters, the reader has traversed the whole course of the essentials in Christian living.

Hebrews and Revelation
You reap extra benefits when you study Hebrews and Revelation together. Together, they become a high-charged study in similarities and contrasts. Each helps to illuminate the content of the other.

First consider the similarities:

1. Each of these books is *sui generis*—in a class of its own. Hebrews does not fit into any other list of letters—neither Paul's nor that of the general epistles. The author is unnamed and unknown. Speculation has surfaced the names of Paul, Barnabas and Apollos, among others. But even if the author were known, it is only with difficulty that we call it a letter at all. Although it ends as a letter might, it begins as an essay or a treatise.

Revelation likewise defies attempts to classify it. What has happened is that all of the highly symbolic, futuristic literature that prophesied a final struggle and end of the age came to be classified as "apocalyptic," after the title of this one unclassifiable book which was known as the "Apocalypse" (or the Revelation) of Jesus Christ to John. Nothing in biblical literature prepares us for what we find in Revelation—not gospel, nor letter, nor Old Testament prophecy. Like the book of Hebrews, it stands alone and is full of surprises. And like Hebrews it has intrigued generations of Bible students, yielding its secret only to those who take account of its substantial uniqueness in the biblical canon.

2. Both Hebrews and Revelation display an exalted image of Christ. It is not the rabbi from Nazareth they see; rather it is the heavenly priest, more glorious than Moses (Heb 3:3), a "ruler of kings on earth" (Rev 1:5), the "glory of God [who] bears the very stamp of his nature" (Heb 1:3), "the Alpha and the Omega . . . who is and who was and who is to come, the Almighty" (Rev 1:8).

3. Both exalt the place of believers. In Hebrews believers are shown to take part in the glory and honor of Christ as brothers and sisters (Heb 2:11). Revelation shows the martyrs reigning with Christ for a thousand years (Rev 20:4-6).

4. Both have an underlying theme, namely, that the faithfulness of Christ calls for the faithfulness of believers.

5. Finally, both emphasize the final, complete and unalterable victory of Christ. For Hebrews that victory is accomplished in the priestly act of sacrifice on the cross. In Revelation that victory is realized in the kingly coronation, judgment and reign of Christ. But for both, what Christ has done is sufficient for all redemption. Nothing can be added, nothing taken away. It is superabundant salvation.

Now, however, note the remarkable contrasts:

1. In Revelation the figure of Christ is the king who reigns; in Hebrews he is the priest who intercedes. In Revelation he represents God to man; in Hebrews, he represents man before God.

2. In Revelation we see the holiness of Christ in contrast to

us. In Hebrews it is the humanity of Christ in common with us.

3. In Revelation the triumph of Christ is gained by his second coming. In Hebrews, the triumph is gained by his first coming.

4. Revelation demonstrates Christ's triumph through divine power and might. For Hebrews, his triumph is won through human suffering and frailty.

5. The atonement in Revelation results in a vision of the absence of a temple that is no longer needed. In Hebrews the tabernacle (as the precursor of the temple) is a central symbol of atonement—though it is a "more perfect tabernacle, not made with hands."

6. In Revelation Christ's victory inaugurates an earthly kingdom. In Hebrews the scene of his victory is a heavenly tabernacle.

7. Last, Revelation relates salvation to the future—it is envisioned and fulfilled in the time of the end of all things. Hebrews relates Christ's victory to the historical past—there Christ's victory is accomplished and promised in the price paid at Golgotha.

New Testament Study: The Key

Ian Robinson said "a language of religion can always be destroyed in one generation."[8] His remark may be true of religious language—or religious understanding—in general. But one thing gives the sacred Scriptures of the Christian faith an unusual staying power. That is the New Testament—a packet of letters and small documents easily accessible to any who will take the trouble to read it. And once we have arrived at a reasonable order and sequence of study, it is almost as if the scales fall from our eyes and the world of the Bible spreads out before us. This testament is the touchstone of religious language and understanding.

6
How to
Read the
Old Testament

———————

Why are people so often hesitant to get into the Old Testament and really *read* it? (Read it, that is, as opposed to choosing a small section for a lesson text.) I suspect the answer has a lot to do with culture shock.

The New Testament is easier because it is more familiar. It is true that in Matthew we could have felt an alien wind blowing across the pages. Along with James, Hebrews and Revelation, it was animated by that strange and distant spirit of ancient oriental culture. But, apart from these four books, the New Testament is comparatively Western. It seems to speak our language. The forms of literature do not puzzle us; they are letters, portraits and history for the most part. And the one book that does puzzle us the most is the one that springs most directly from the ancient Palestinian world—Revelation.

But the Old Testament is not so easy. There is history, but it's not the kind we studied in a freshman course in Western Civilization. Some of it looks at first like history, but turns out to be poetry or drama, like Job. There are aphorisms and songs, essays and prophecies. The prophecies are for the most part written by prophets, but sometimes they are written about the prophet, as in Jonah. They are mostly addressed to the people of God, but sometimes they are addressed to God himself, as Habakkuk did in his writing.

For a dozen reasons the ground is less certain beneath our feet. Many things are strange and questionable. The morality is one example. Samson gets up from the bed of a harlot and then is embued with power from on high to carry off the gates of Gaza. Samuel tells Saul that it is the will of God for every man, woman and child of the Amalekites to be slain. When the king is spared, he rises in holy wrath against Saul, prophesies against him and hews Amalek to pieces. These things hardly lead us to thoughts of the Sermon on the Mount. Ulfilas, the fourth-century missionary to the Goths, thought it best in his translation of the Bible for these warlike people to leave out the books of Samuel and Kings altogether, knowing that his people would be unduly attracted to the bloody affairs of Hebrew warriors.

Old Testament Authority
In spite of these features that create a certain timidity about the Old Testament and a feeling of disorientation on our part, we can have no doubt that the New Testament writers—all of them—and Jesus himself saw the Old Testament as bedrock authority. Furthermore, in the Old Testament they found confirmation of the new covenant that was dawning upon them. The New Testament was never entirely new; it was the reiteration of those things that had been pointed out, hinted at and expected in the Old.

Jesus said, "You search the scriptures; . . . and it is they that bear witness to me" (Jn 5:39). Paul finds, as wholly sufficient to his argument, the fact that Old Testament scripture is in agreement. When Paul argues, for instance, that one is justified "by faith apart from works of law" (Rom 3:28), he appeals to the Genesis witness that Abraham was counted righteous before his circumcision and in view of his faith:

We say that faith was reckoned to Abraham as righteousness. How then was it reckoned to him? Was it before or after he

had been circumcised? It was not after, but before he was circumcised. He received circumcision as a sign or seal of the righteousness which he had by faith while he was still uncircumcised. (Rom 4:9-11)
The New Testament, then, does not stand on its own; it never did and it never will. It goes beyond the Old Testament. But it does not transcend it in the sense that the new covenant makes the old covenant obsolete. Instead it fulfills, continues and embodies those great themes found in the old books of Israel.

There is nothing that Jesus made more clear or emphasized more strongly than the fact that his teachings did not *replace* or *repeal* the older inspired teaching:

Think not that I have come to abolish the law and the prophets; I have come not to abolish them but to fulfil them. For truly, I say to you, till heaven and earth pass away, not an iota, not a dot, will pass from the law until all is accomplished. (Mt 5:17-18)

The Key Difference

You can find a clue, however, to the best way to read the Old Testament when you find the point of greatest difference between the two testaments.

The main difference is this: the New Testament focuses on one solid, compact, historical event; the Old Testament deals with many varied events. The New Testament finds that one event to be inexhaustible in its meaning and intentions. The Old Testament finds a few basic themes to be reiterated and reinforced in the many events of history. For the New Testament the many themes are pulled together by one central event. In the Old Testament, however, the few basic themes pull together the myriad history-making events.

Therefore the point of interest in New Testament study is to see how the one supreme event of the life, ministry, death and resurrection of Christ is *illuminated* by the enormously rich conclusions that are drawn from it. In the Old Testament, however, we need to locate those few *themes* that are *illustrated* over and over again in history.

Once those themes are discovered, then we begin to see them everywhere. They give us a key to the grammar of the Old Testament.

For instance, one theme found throughout the prophets is a stress on the superiority of obedience over the cultic sacrifice of lambs and bulls. The theme stands out clearly in Isaiah, Jeremiah, Hosea and Micah. But without a sense of that theme it may be hard to know what to make of the story of Saul piously sacrificing the burnt offering at Gilgal and then gaining the holy wrath of Samuel and losing his dynasty.

Saul was about to go out and fight Philistines. According to the mind of his day, religious acts were to prompt cooperation from the gods. Samuel, the legitimate priest, was not there to do the "religious" thing, and so Saul felt the need to do it himself. The conflict, therefore, was over just this point: Was the sacrifice done in obedience to God and therefore according to his prescription? Or was it done presumptuously in order to enlist God's aid against the Philistines? At the heart of the matter is this principle that God is not swayed by cultic practices, but he demands obedience. This inward disposition of the heart toward faithfulness, as opposed to the outward sacrifice devoid of sincerity, is a prophetic theme that unlocks a dozen or more doors into the chambers of Old Testament thought.

Therefore I believe the most fruitful approach to Old Testament study is to make ourselves aware of the most prominent and obvious themes. Briefly, I want to summarize a few major themes you should look for in the Old Testament. The list can be expanded into a score of subthemes, but if I concentrate on those matters that are essential and distinctive, I think we can do justice by looking at four prominent and comprehensive Old Testament truths.

These four might be listed as four brief, but intense and comprehensive, Old Testament convictions:

1. One God has created all things good.

2. Evil is contrary to God's will, and it is therefore a perversion of the true order of things.

3. God has elected his people for his redemptive purposes.

4. God intends to redeem his creation in justice and love.

There we have the comprehensive sweep of the Old Testament. These are themes that rise to the surface again and again, giving an inner purpose to all the particulars of life. Creation, the Fall, election, redemption—these are the points on which all the history, prophecies, wisdom and poetry of the Old Testament turn.

A person has begun to learn the Old Testament when each of these four themes calls to mind a cluster of stories, sayings and prophecies, all of which add to the weight and substance of these fundamental convictions.

The Lord God Is One

It has been said that the oneness of God is the only dogma of Israel. No doubt this is the highest truth, without which all of the others lose their meaning. The central prayer of the Hebrew religion was, and continues to be, the *Shema*, which repeats "Hear, O Israel: The LORD our God is one LORD; and you shall love the LORD your God with all your heart, and with all your soul, and with all your might" (Deut 6:4-5). A five-year-old Jewish schoolchild learns this confession as his first lesson; he repeats it at the time of feasting and in time of mourning, and he hopes to have that sentence on his lips at the last waking moment of life. Rabbi Pinchas Lapide says that "what the 'Shema Israel' has meant for the inner life and survival of Judaism can only with difficulty be understood from without."[1]

It is probably true that Israel was not monotheistic, in the modern sense of that word, from its earliest days. It is likely that Israel moved over the centuries from henotheism (the belief that their God was the highest of all gods) to monolatry (the worship of one God exclusively) to true monotheism (the belief that there is only one true God). Nevertheless, the *principle* of monotheism is there from the earliest times—even if the people of that day would not have expressed it as would a John Wesley or a C. S. Lewis. And that implicit monotheism, held against all odds by a few prophets in a small Mediterranean nation, developed in its Palestinian chrysalis and hung by a slender thread for centuries until it exploded all over the Mediterranean world through the Christian gospel, leaving that world never again the same.

At the beginning of the first century the world was a world of many powers and many gods. Even though Egypt had seen a short season of speculative monotheism and Babylon may have as well, the living worship of one God was a minuscule minority practice. Only because of God's providence and the fierce insistence of a few Hebrew prophets did this light not flicker out in the great sea of pagan religions. The Old Testament, in part, is the story of how that miracle of perseverance happened.

But the bare conviction of *only one God* is not where the Old Testament leaves the matter. It is not only the idea of God that changes, it is the concept of human nature and of the world that changes with it. Here is the secret behind the change that took place as the world moved from the paganism of the first century to the widespread Christian belief in one God only a few centuries later.

In the first place monotheism demands that God's character be stamped on all creation and that it be the standard for all action. The pagan world is a patchwork of divine powers, each with limited authority. The world created by the one God is a unity, altogether dependent on the one God. The world of pagan multiplicity of gods is also a world with a multiplicity of peoples with no common existence, because their highest objects of worship go no farther than the tribal boundaries. The God of the monotheist, by the necessity of logic, belongs to all people, and all people belong to him. The idea of a common humanity sprang from the belief in one God.

Monotheism leads not only to a unity of being, it leads also to a unity of ethical standards. The idea of one God, says Lapide, is not simply a quantitative idea; it is a qualitative one:

> Two or more cannot be absolute. Two or more also cannot be timeless and eternal. If there are two or more, there can be no concept of omnipotence. Two or more must lead to a division of labor and to conflict; likewise, where the recep-

tion of "only two" is present as by Zoroaster, the lordship will be divided between good and evil, with devastating effects in popular belief. For what the one bids, the other can forbid; what Zeus commands, Hera can sabotage—thus monotheism also becomes an indispensable presupposition of a mono-ethics.[2]

When we open the Old Testament, the conviction of one God, one world, one standard of justice, one Lord of all life comes at us from every side. "In the beginning God created the heavens and the earth"—everything. The epic struggle between Elijah and the advocates of the fertility gods sets the tone for all of the history of prophetism. In the contest at Mount Carmel with the priests of Baal, Elijah taunts the priests, suggesting that their god is preoccupied, temporarily out of the office or asleep. From the ironic tone it is clear that the prophet believes that Baal is no god at all. The text gives it away. When the priests of Baal had shouted, cut themselves with knives and limped around the altar all morning long, the writer comments: "But there was no voice, and no one answered" (1 Kings 18:26). Clearly, the conviction had grown to a powerful confidence that these other so-called gods are no gods at all. Every power that is finds its source in the one true God—the God who had graciously revealed himself to Israel.

The earliest expressions of monotheism are simple and straightforward without the refinements given to it by later revelation. From our later perspective we are sometimes shocked to find that God is a God of war; the power to overcome enemies, like all of the important powers, emanates from God. Therefore the one God of Israel absorbs all of the gross attributes of the wars of that time, with its total destruction of men, women and children (although one might wonder why that should especially shock twentieth-century people). We also find it strange that, in the case of Saul's madness, the first book of Samuel says he was sent an evil spirit from the Lord (as, for example, 1 Samuel 19:9).

Revelation waits for later developments before these problems come into focus, but one idea becomes loud and clear—

even too intensely shrill for us who have now taken the point for granted—and that is the belief that all powers, all creation, all existence derive from the one God. No longer is there *any* being or *any* power that lives independently of God. What to do with the problem of evil they had not yet discovered. But what they *had* discovered set everything else on its head: one God rules all nature, all peoples, all history. If there are evil spirits, then they too, like all else, cannot be independent of God. The powers of war, as well as the powers of peace belong to the one God. First, all of these contending powers had to be swept from the landscape: to this aim the pre-exilic prophets dedicated the deepest passions of their lives.

Only because they did make this point stick—only because they would sooner die than give in to the popular paganism of most of their countrymen—and only because this was established as first principle in the Scriptures that have now covered the world, are we now able to think of a world with a common hope. Unity of every kind began with the realization that "in the beginning God created heaven and earth."

The Good Creation
Linked to that idea is the coordinating conviction that when God created all things, all things bore the mark of his character, and therefore all creation was good—just as God himself is good. To the question "What is the nature of this life?"—Is it benevolent, malevolent or indifferent?—the Old Testament never gives a hint that it could really be anything but benevolent. "And God saw everything that he had made, and behold, it was very good" (Gen 1:31).

But that leaves us with a problem. If we believe that God created all and that he created it good, then to explain the existence of evil we are left with a limited number of options within monotheism.

The Old Testament Confronts Evil
Unlike many of its modern interpreters, the Bible takes the matter of evil altogether seriously and realistically. John Crowe

Ransom notes that "the Old Testament is a book provided plentifully with intense lamentations. In the world's literature the Hebrew scriptures are doubtless as woeful as any other document, not excepting Dante's epic or Shakespeare's tragedies."[3]

But what is this evil and where does it come from? If there were two or more gods, we could simply assign evil to the operation of one of the gods. But since God is one and God is good, evil has no place to reside. Some solve this dilemma by saying that evil is an illusion, and God alone is real; Christian Scientists are not the only ones to have dealt with this problem by consigning illness and other evils to the realm of unreality. Ransom laments the fact that the "new religionists would have their cake and eat it too. . . . They want One Great God, yet they want him to be wholly benevolent, and ethical after the humane definition. What will they do about evil? . . . They will do nothing about it . . . as a temporary, incidental, negligible, and slightly uncomfortable phenomenon, which hardly deserves an entry in the theological ledger."[4]

Others solve this dilemma, as Bertrand Russell did, by admitting the reality of evil but denying the reality of God. The argument would run that if God is the monotheistic God of the Jews and Christians, who stands alone responsible for the universe of things and events, then he would have all sovereignty. With unlimited power he could eliminate evil—both physical evil such as illness and disasters and moral evil. But he does not do so; therefore, he does not exist.

The Bible, however, while never questioning the reality of God, takes with full seriousness the reality of evil. It gives evil a place that is not on the same level with that of the positive reality of creation. Evil is not seen as part of the creation itself. Rather it grows out of a moral disposition. It is not natural frailty that has undone us, nor ignorance, nor the fates, nor our mortality. The problem lies in our refusal to do that which we know is right.

Therefore we see this matter very differently than we do other things in the world. Evil is not *some thing* as much as it is the *lack of something*.

The comparison is not unlike that of sickness and health. A man visits the doctor for a checkup and the doctor says: "You are not in good health. You are fifteen pounds overweight, your pulse rate is too fast, and you need to bring down your blood pressure." What qualifies the doctor to make such a judgment that his patient is not in good health? It is because he is supposed to know the signs of good physical condition. *A diagnosis of illness only makes sense in connection with the idea of health.*

It is the same with the idea of evil. Evil, with its roots in sin, is not a part of creation. It is a disorder that is deep-rooted and persistent, but its reality consists only in that it distorts and falls short of God's intention for his good creation. Just as illness is the degree to which someone lacks good health, sin is a condition that deprives us of a good, full and wholesome life. It is not something in itself; it is something gone wrong. It is a spoiled relationship, a misguided love, a destructive hatred, an unhealthy desire, a defective faith, a distortion of the truth.

A definition of sin can become more specific, but its essence is the same. The rabbis said that the number of commandments in the Bible (Old Testament) is 613; therefore a sin is a deviation from any of these 613 laws. Behind this definition, however, is the belief that God had given the law—and any transgression of the law was, at heart, rebellion against God.

The Bible describes sin as a loss of relatedness to God and, therefore, to creation and to the rest of humanity as well. Cain cries out that his sin and punishment is more than he can bear: "Behold, thou hast driven me this day away from the ground; and from thy face I shall be hidden; and I shall be a fugitive and a wanderer on the earth, and whoever finds me will slay me" (Gen 4:14). He is alienated from nature, from God and from his fellow human beings. Thus the nature of sin is shown to be the loss of proper relationship. The extreme and appropriate expression of this condition is death. Sin is a rebellion against God, therefore against his order, and therefore against being itself. C. S. Lewis commented on this condition by saying that the story of the Fall is one in which "man asked for rebellion, and God gave it to him." Humanity rebelled against God, so all of creation rebelled against humanity.

But in all of these aspects we see that sin describes, not a thing that has an independent reality of its own, but a condition that is out of harmony with the order of life and therefore tends to diminish existence. The Hebrew word for sin is *hattath,* which is translated to the Greek *hamartia* (in the Septuagint and in the New Testament). Both the Hebrew and the Greek words derive from verbs meaning simply "to miss the mark." Sin is, therefore, a distortion and a diminishing of what should be. It is real, but it is reality losing its virtue and losing its power against nothingness. It is life, but it is cancerous life that ends in destruction of the organism. It is activity, but it is misdirected and destructive; and because it is the refusal to act right, it soon forfeits the ability to act at all. That is why so many of the prophets could subscribe to the adage "Sin is suicidal."

God's Purpose and God's People
An impersonal age like our own finds great comfort in generalizations and abstractions. The individual is somehow lost in all of this. We have heroes, or even superstars, but this adulation is based on some abstracted talent or quality that has little to do with the whole person. An athlete can be known across the nation for the feats he performs on Sunday afternoon and for the astronomical salary that he draws; it makes little difference that his personal life is coming apart at the seams. "Stars" are abstracted images created by the movie industry, the music industry, and by a host of attendant media. They are celebrities, but not persons. The real man or woman who happens to be the object of this public acclaim—which goes no deeper than the groove on an LP album—occasionally complains of the invasion of privacy.

Privacy! Up to that point the public had given the star's privacy less than a moment's thought—and they still have trouble taking it seriously. After all, privacy or the demand for privacy only makes sense when a real soul, with its deeper mysteries and its unpublic side, is at stake. Celluloid images have no

souls; only real people do. When images object, it is startling—
as if something spoke up which was assumed to be mute. Abstractions are not expected to be so motivated.

The Old Testament has little interest in pushing generalities
or abstractions, but it is absorbed with interest in individuals,
concrete individuals with names and families and personal histories. Who are the elect? Even the great concept of God's
universal concern only comes slowly into view; it lies beneath
the surface from the earliest times. But this is the consuming
interest of Israel's religion: God is the "God of Abraham, Isaac
and Jacob." Men with souls, whole men, who had a hidden
side—even a dark side—who often rebelled wholeheartedly
before they surrendered as men overcome by love: these are
the subjects of the Old Testament.

But that is why the Old Testament often strikes us as peculiar
and difficult to understand. It would be easier if we could trans-
late the story of God's providence into a general movement of
history. Marxists habitually speak of "forces of history"—no
one is sure what such a magical "force" is, but somehow it still
sounds convincing. We might have no objection if the Bible
dealt with "structures of society" or "power structures." Magical
and ghostly as that word *structure* might be, our age can make
good use of it since it sounds general, abstract and therefore
scientific.

I don't denigrate the necessity of abstractions; we can't think
at all without them. But my point is that if we put styles of
thinking on a line from "mostly concrete" to "mostly abstract,"
then, although our century would lean toward abstractions, the
Old Testament comes down clearly on the side of the concrete.

That is why the stories of the Old Testament circulate around
specific men and women. God's redemptive work did not begin
with a "plan of salvation," but with Abraham and his specific,
personal history. The threat of a tide of paganism was not
turned back by an abstraction of historical conditions, but by
Elijah, whom God hurled into the conflict. It was not a general
deliverance, much less a philosophy of deliverance, that the
Jews expected, but a Deliverer, a Messiah.

That is why the concept of election in the Old Testament means more than God's choosing someone or other to carry out his mission. It is all wrapped up with the mystery of concrete persons, with distinct personalities. As God elects them, he also reveals something about himself. We discover more about God because of what we see in Elijah—not simply in what he did, but in who he was, what he hated and what he loved. The zeal of Elijah tells us who Elijah was, but more importantly, that passion reflects the God he worshiped.

Israel was elected—both the man and the nation. That election changed Israel—as much the nation as the man, and in that change we begin to discover God as Jeremiah or Isaiah knew him. The prophets knew God's justice (Amos) and his mercy (Hosea), but how God affected their lives tells us more about God than abstract propositions on justice and mercy.

Abraham Heschel's comments here reflect this view of the Bible:

The Bible is primarily not man's vision of God but God's vision of man. The Bible is not man's theology but God's anthropology, dealing with man and what He asks of him rather than with the [abstract] nature of God. God did not reveal to the prophets eternal mysteries but His knowledge and love of man. It was not the aspiration of Israel to know the Absolute but to ascertain what He asks of man; to commune with His will rather than His essence.[5]

That is of first importance in the meaning of election.

The God of Redemption
The fourth theme is that God desires and intends to redeem us.

The word *gaal* (to redeem) in the Old Testament world was full of real-life associations. A debtor is forced to sell his property to satisfy his debt, but his next of kin is obligated to buy back the property for him—he redeems the property (Lev 25:25). He has no property, so he sells himself into slavery— and his next of kin redeems him (Lev 25:47-49). In Isaiah's Book of Comfort (chapters 40-66) God is Israel's "next of kin."

Redemption implies being released from bondage. And it
means being restored to a condition that is more desirable.
Those who had been sold to sin, bound to a condition of death
are now set free in order to live. The need for redemption
implies that we are in a worse condition now than formerly, but
when we are restored, it is to a better condition than ever
before. Thus Paul, who was well acquainted with the Old Testament, wanted to restore Onesimus to Philemon, but no longer
as a slave, rather as a brother in Christ. Onesimus was saved
from a fate that could have meant death. Now Paul was arguing
not that he be restored as a servant in good standing, but that
he be welcomed as a free man.

One thing the Old Testament helps us to see is the results
of this redemption. If people are redeemed to a better life, then
what is the nature of that life? For the Old Testament believer
it might mean that the crops would grow, the flocks and herds
would increase, and the enemy would be destroyed. The purpose of religion was to order conditions in such a way that the
person need not change. That is one way of viewing religion,
and H. L. Mencken evidently thought that was the only way.
"There is nothing really secret or complex about it," he said.
"Whether it happens to show itself in the artless mumbo-jumbo
of a Winnebago Indian or in the elaborately refined and meta-
physical rites of a Christian archbishop, its single function is to
give man access to the powers which seem to control his destiny, and its single purpose is to induce those powers to be
friendly to him. . . . Nothing else is essential."[6]

Others might think of redemption as protection from the
fearful prospects of life—and especially the prospect of death.
The Egyptians and the Babylonians were absorbed with the
goal of immortality. Israel was ringed with people who made
special provisions for the dead and prepared themselves for life
in the hereafter. But Old Testament faith strangely has little to
say about life after death. The kernel of a doctrine of life after
death is there, but it is hardly a full-blown, well-developed conviction.

Israel is absorbed with *this* world, *this* life, and leaves the afterlife in the dark shadows of mystery. What they *do* say about immortality, both in the Old Testament and later, comes because of a peculiar preoccupation. Redemption for Israel was not the manipulation of nature and circumstances, not the overcoming of death, but being brought back to a condition of fellowship with God. And that fellowship could only be restored if men and women themselves changed.

The root problem, as we have seen, is sin. It is the fact that although we know what is right, we do not do it. Therefore the passion of Israel was for righteousness; it was to know and to love and to perform the will of God. Man erred through disobedience; now he could only be restored through obedience. If God is the creator and sovereign of all things, then the only proper, realistic and possible relationship with him is through obedience.

The whole force of the Old Testament teaching, then, goes forth from this point: we need to be made righteous; we cannot live otherwise; and only God has the power to make us righteous. H. Wheeler Robinson states in his *Religious Ideas of the Old Testament:*

> The Old Testament is undoubtedly the most profoundly moral book which antiquity can offer. Its moral emphasis cannot be adequately represented by the quotation of a number of striking verses, such as Micah's "What doth Yahweh require of thee, but to do justly, and to love mercy, and to walk humbly with thy God?" Similar utterances selected from the literatures of other religions would not prove that they possessed Israel's emphasis on morality. This is shown rather by the part which moral ideas have taken in the development of the religion, notably in the prophetic teaching of the eighth century.[7]

Illustrating his point that morality is the heart of Old Testament religion, Wheeler Robinson draws support from Amos, the words of Nathan to David concerning Bathsheba, the words of Elijah to Ahab regarding the vineyard of Naboth, from the Pentateuch and from the wisdom literature. Then he goes on, "When Hosea argues from the moral relations between his

adulterous wife and himself to those between Israel and Yah-
weh, the principle involved was more important than that
which Newton discovered when he linked a falling apple to a
moving star. It made a spiritual pathway along which thought
could move and did move with confidence."[8]

Matthew Arnold makes the point forcefully in his *Literature
and Dogma*. He grants the point that all people have arrived at
a morality, and basically the same morality. But the remarkable
thing about the Old Testament is that the morality, which was
the common sense of the people, was married to and empowered by religion. Religion was power and emotion. Morality
might be related to this religion, but it need not be.

The primitive and nontheist world is full of examples where
morality, or conduct, hardly defines the essence of religious
life. Morality may, indeed often does, play a part in the religious
life, but the distractions of that nonmoral element in religion
are many. "Only with one people," Arnold said, "the people
from whom we get the Bible,—these distractions did not happen." He goes on, in an extraordinary passage:

The Old Testament, nobody will ever deny, is filled with the
word and thought of righteousness. "In the way of righteousness is life, and in the pathway thereof is no death;" "He that
pursueth evil pursueth it to his own death;" "The way of
transgressors is hard;"—nobody will deny that those texts
may stand for the fundamental and ever-recurring idea of
the Old Testament. No people ever felt so strongly as the
people of the Old Testament, the Hebrew people, that conduct is three-fourths of our life and its largest concern. No
people ever felt so strongly that succeeding, going right, hit-
ting the mark in this great concern, was *the way of peace*, the
highest possible satisfaction. "He that keepeth the law, happy
is he; its ways are ways of pleasantness, and all its paths are
peace; if thou hadst walked in its ways, thou shouldst have
dwelt in peace for ever!" Jeshurun, one of the ideal names
of their race, is the *upright*; Israel, the other and greater, is
the *wrestler with God*, he who has known the contention and
strain it costs to stand upright. That mysterious personage by

whom their history first touches the hill of Sion, is Melchi-
sedek, the *righteous* king. Their holy city, Jerusalem, is the
foundation, or vision, or inheritance, of that which righteousness achieves—*peace.* The law of righteousnes was such
an object of attention to them, that its words were to "be in
their hearts, and thou shalt teach them diligently unto thy
children, and shalt talk of them when thou sittest in thine
house, and when thou walkest by the way, and when thou
liest down, and when thou risest up." That they might keep
them ever in mind, they wore them, went about with them,
made talismans of them. "Bind them upon thy fingers, bind
them about thy neck; write them upon the table of thine
heart!" "Take fast hold of her," they said of the doctrine of
conduct, or righteousness, "let her not go! keep her, for *she
is thy life!*"[9]

Standing behind the great theme of redemption, then, is the
massive conviction on the part of Israel that what humanity is
called back to, what it is redeemed for, is a life of right action,
right thought, right affection—righteousness.

John the Baptist, following in the tradition of the Old Testament prophets called for repentance leading to the remis-
sion—the sending away—of sin. But, in addition, he pointed
toward that one who would "baptize you with the Holy Spirit"
(Lk 3:16). The New Testament announced the new power to
achieve that for which the Old Testament established the need.
But of first importance was convincing the world—or at least
the world of Israel—that humanity's supreme need was to order
its life in harmony with a righteous God. It would hardly be an
exaggeration to say that the writings of the Old Testament
prophets—if not the Old Testament itself—was an extended
exercise in defining righteousness, in teaching the way of righteousness, and in exalting a supernaturally empowered passion
for righteousness.

The Secret of Thematic Study
What strikes me forcefully about the Old Testament is how
these few themes are given to us in a thousand ways. They are

embedded in law, they are sung by singers, they are portrayed in drama, they are turned into proverbs by sages. These same messages (few but intense) become the obsessions of prophets—something that a surfeited and materialistic age little understands since obsessive moral vision seldom happens in controlled environments where discomforts are kept to a minimum. These prophets, single-eyed in pursuit of narrow but intense preoccupations, lifted their voices in the shrine at Bethel, acted out their visions in the streets of Jerusalem, shouted out warnings to Nineveh, held out consolation to enslaved Israel, and risked death before kings and violent censure before crowds.

These few themes became the subjects of their dreams, their visions, their marriages, their births, their hopes, their fears, their certainties and their doubts. For these few truths they were stoned, exiled, threatened and isolated from society. Isaiah showed the sovereignty of God when he prophesied Jerusalem's safety in spite of the siege from Assyria. Jeremiah did the same when he forecast Jerusalem's fall. And when Jerusalem stood secure against the awesome Assyrian army, that proved the sovereignty of God. And when, more than a century later, it fell to the Babylonians, it proved the same point.

The themes weave to and fro into intricate patterns. Here they stand out forcefully in bright hues; there they are subtle shades but richer and deeper. The focus of submission to God is loyalty to the chosen nation in Ezra, and it is kindness to a stranger in Ruth. God's justice comes down in righteous wrath on Nineveh in the prophecies of Nahum, but Jonah's prophecy brings God's mercy. Ezekiel dreams of a temple rebuilt as an assurance of the presence of God; Jeremiah envisions a time when God's presence is so real that the ark of the covenant— that holiest relic of the temple—will not be sought out or missed. Proverbs assures God's faithfulness to those who are righteous; Job says God's faithfulness goes beyond the rewards of the moment. He is faithful even when by all appearances he seems not to be.

These themes grow and develop throughout the Old Testa-

ment. Sometimes they are eclipsed by a new discovery, as when
Ezra's concern for purity tended to obscure the universality of
God's love, or when the loving-kindness of Hosea left behind
the awe-filled righteousness of God in Amos. But the themes
rise and fall. They display new facets and open up new applications. A part of this richness of the Old Testament is that it
is displayed through a variety of forms of expression. Only
through a diversity of literature is the full range of these ideas
or themes expressed.

The secret of reading the Old Testament is not so much in
attending to the myriad details, but in attending to the long-
running themes, those great rivers that begin with tributaries in
the earlier books of Israel's history and become broad rivers in
the great books of Isaiah and Jeremiah and Malachi. The details are important, but they tend to adhere to the themes once
these great central convictions are recognized.

The Old Testament Symphony

The variety of the Old Testament books—history, poetry and
prophecy—has its effect on the themes and on your reading of
the themes. The Old Testament is like a symphony with one
theme but several movements. The many instruments and different movements give the musical theme new and varied interpretations. The violin section will sound quite different from
the piano, or from the brass and percussion. But the theme is
the same—or is it?

Doesn't the theme itself take on new depth, new richness and
new meaning because of the instruments that interpret it and
the variations between movements? The same is true of the
themes of the Old Testament. The few themes branch out into
many interpretations through a symphony of writers, speakers
and forms.

The work of Old Testament readers is to continue seeing and
ferreting out the ageless themes in the varying literary forms,
in the manifold histories, and in the wisdom that speaks a
language strangely distant and foreign. To do that, we must
listen to the theme in the language that the particular writing

presents. If it is poetry, then we must not look for descriptive history, but must see the theme as poetry would express it. If it is primeval history, the story of the creation and fall, then we must be satisfied with stories very different from those in yesterday's newspaper—truer, no doubt!—but also less *descriptive* and more *prescriptive*. They are stories meant not so much to satisfy our curiosities as to help us see how things are *now*, and to call us back to a God-given purpose and destiny.

The variations in these ancient documents—so much a part of the difficulty in Old Testament reading—must be rescued from their role as barriers and be seen as aids. They are the true friends of those who genuinely want to understand the lessons of the Old Testament. The reason? It is simply that this grammar of faith, which the Old Testament teaches, is taught, not once and not even three times, but with all the variety, all the reiteration, all the redoubled literary force that the Old Testament itself represents. What appears to be our most formidable foe when we begin our reading turns out, in the long run, to be our firmest ally.

7
Individual
Book
Study

It is with books as with men," said Voltaire, "a very small number play a great part."

I wonder if Voltaire, that great detractor of the Bible, felt the enormous irony of his words. After all, any really honest listing of influential books must be headed by the Bible. And not only that, but of all the others that had "played a great part" hardly any could match the influence of any one of the sixty-six books of the Bible.

It is on those individual books that we now focus. Here is the real unit of the Bible—not the verse, nor the chapter, nor the larger sections. The Bible was written in books; or, we might better say, these letters, Gospels and prophecies were written long before, from a human perspective, the Bible as a whole was ever in view. And since the writing took place with only the single book in mind, it is only reasonable that this should also be our real unit of study. Bible study takes root here or it does not take root at all.

Methods must be adapted to the type of book we are reading. But there are a few general guidelines that will help.

Book Study in Five Steps

As for all Bible study, the rule proves true here: *simplicity is a great ally.* The subject matter often becomes complex enough—especially if you are reading Isaiah, Jeremiah or Romans. The object of any study method should be to break down complexity, to simplify.

The method I suggest here is comprised of three complete readings of a book. Each reading involves a somewhat different procedure. The first reading is the broadest survey, and the third reading is the closest and most detailed study. We move from the general to the particular, from the broad picture to the careful, detailed study.

This can be accomplished in five successive steps:

Step One: First Reading—Overview
Step Two: Preparation for Second Reading
Step Three: Second Reading—Outline
Step Four: Preparation for Third Reading
Step Five: Third Reading—Analysis

Now let's see how these steps work out in detail.

First Reading—Overview

Read the book through in one sitting if possible. For most books in the Old and New Testaments, a reading that takes place all in one sitting is well within reason. Some—like Isaiah and Jeremiah—might require more time than you can give to one reading. In that case, break the text up into two or three readings—or, at least, into as few readings as seems practical.

The object of this first reading is to get an overview. Your aim is a broad and undetailed acquaintance with the book—just the sort of impression that the original writer would have expected of his first readers. If we can assume that he intended to communicate the first time, then we must expect to see the basic lines of his thought in our first, immediate sweep of the writing.

Read as follows:

☐ Keep in mind that the writer had a purpose, or sometimes more than one purpose, for writing this letter, Gospel or prophecy. Search for that purpose or theme as you read.

☐ Note the character of the book. What kind of literature is it? Is it history? Is it a prophecy? Is it primarily poetry or prose? Or is it, like Isaiah, printed with long sections of poetic verse and long sections of prose? Is it a letter? If so, to whom is it written? and for what occasion?

☐ Mentally, note those topics, terms and expressions that seem to recur again and again in the writing.

☐ Do not take notes at this point. Underline or mark important passages in the margin so you can return to these and give them a closer reading. The aim here is to engage in a fairly rapid, uninterrupted reading. Taking notes interrupts the flow of the sentences and paragraphs.

☐ Remember that the purpose of this first reading is to let the book communicate to us in an immediate sense. Naturally there is much that you will miss, and it will necessarily keep you from poring over certain passages that seem to invite you to stop and look them up in a commentary. But these other concerns, such as background, definition of terms and the careful inspection of the writer's thought, can wait for a later, closer reading. One immediate concern is to gain an overall framework, so that the close details can be placed within an already familiar context.

☐ Before you begin reading a book, look over the questions listed below. Keep these in mind as you read the text. When you complete the first reading answer as many of these as possible.

Questions for the First Reading
1. What is the title?
2. Who is the author (if that can be known by reading the book)?
3. What is (are) the main theme(s)?
4. What words or phrases or statements occur frequently in the writing?
5. In addition to the main theme, what are other significant points in the book?
6. What is the tone of the writing? (Joyful, wrathful, full of hope, fear, uncertainty, courage, confidence?)
7. What is your immediate personal response? (How does it

make you feel? What does it make you think about?)

8. What does it teach about behavior or ethics?

9. What other features impress you in this particular book?

Do not attempt to answer these questions until after you have read the entire book. The first reading, then, becomes a two-step process: (1) Read the book, freely and with as little interruption as possible between beginning and end. And (2) reflect on what you have read by answering these nine questions. (Or, make up your own questions: the point is to systematically prod yourself into thinking about the material you have read.)

Preparation for Second Reading

Select a notebook—loose-leaf, spiral bound, stenographers pad or any that you would find convenient for keeping notes on your reading. Keep it in a convenient place along with your Bible.

Establish a brief outline to guide your second reading. One way to accomplish this is by looking at each paragraph of the text and assigning to each a brief heading or a number. This is preferable to following chapter divisions, since they so frequently interrupt the real paragraphs or thought units of the writer.

Mark your text with the paragraph numbers or headings. Or, writing in your notebook, space out the headings or numbers and allow room to write a few notes in the spaces between.

Another way to give yourself the same guide for a second reading is to borrow an outline. Most study Bibles suggest an outline at the beginning of the text or within the printing of the text itself.

There are traditional or typical divisions of books. A sketch of these outlines can usually be found in Bible dictionaries or commentaries in the general introductory articles on particular books. For instance, Isaiah is typically divided into eight books:

Eight Divisions of Isaiah

I. Book of Rebukes and Promises 1:1—6:13

II. Book of Immanuel 7:1—12:6

III. Book of Foreign Prophecies 13:1—23:18

IV. First Book of General Judgment 24:1—27:13
V. Book of Zion 28:1—33:24
VI. Second Book of General Judgment 34:1—35:10
VII. Book of Hezekiah 36:1—39:8
VIII. Book of Comfort 40:1—66:24

Sometimes the way a book is outlined immediately tells us something about the book. Matthew is an intriguing example. It is made up of alternating sections of narration and teaching, and each double section ends with a standard phrase, such as "when Jesus had finished these sayings . . ." The whole book begins with a prologue and ends with an epilogue. The greater part of Matthew, then, is composed of five "books." We are instantly reminded that the first readership of this Gospel were Jewish Christians, who would have recognized in Matthew an imitation of the *Torah*.

A great prophecy, highly important to the Jews of the first century who expected a Messiah, was Deuteronomy 18:18: "I will raise up for them a prophet like you [Moses] from among their brethren." Here in the very structure of Matthew is the hint that Jesus fulfilled the messianic hope for another and greater Moses. Like the books of Moses themselves, the Gospel displays a prologue, five "books" and an epilogue:

The "Books" of Matthew
Prologue: The Advent (1:1—2:23)
I. The Invitation (3:1—7:29)
  A. Narration (3:1—4:25)
  B. Teaching (5:1—7:29)
II. The Discipline (8:1—11:1)
  A. Narration (8:1—9:35)
  B. Teaching (9:36—11:1)
III. The Kingdom (11:2—13:53)
  A. Narration (11:2—12:50)
  B. Teaching (13:1-53)
IV. The Fellowship (13:53—19:2)
  A. Narration (13:53—17:27)
  B. Teaching (18:1—19:2)
V. The Consummation (19:3—25:46)

A. Narration (19:3—23:39)

B. Teaching (24:1—25:46)

Epilogue: The Passion (26:1—28:20)

The book of Psalms is another that is modeled after the Pentateuch in its fivefold divisions. Most editions of the Psalms make note of each of the five sections. Each book ends with a doxology (for instance, "Blessed be the LORD, the God of Israel, from everlasting to everlasting!" appears at the end of Book I), and the whole of the Psalms ends with the long doxology of Psalm 150.

The Fivefold Psalter

Book I. Psalms 1—41

Book II. Psalms 42—72

Book III. Psalms 73—89

Book IV. Psalms 90—106

Book V. Psalms 107—150

The doxologies are (1) Psalm 41:13, (2) 72:18-19, (3) 89:52, (4) 106:48, and (5) all of 150.

Genesis also has an evident internal pattern if we know what to look for in the text. It is obvious, of course, that Genesis is made up of two large parts: (1) the prologue on universal beginnings (chapters 1—11) and (2) the story of the patriarchs (chapters 12—50). Also, for a long time, people have noticed how the several sections of Genesis each begin with a saying such as, "These are the generations of . . ." The word in Hebrew is *toledoth*—"generation" or "story." Giving attention to what students of Genesis call the "*toledoth* formula" we can see that Genesis is divided by nine *toledoth* sayings, forming ten sections.

The *Toledoth* Sections of Genesis

Universal Beginnings:

1. Creation 1:1—2:4

2. Fall 2:4—4:26

3. Adam and his descendants 5:1-32

4. Noah and the Flood 6:9—9:29

5. Sons of Noah 10:1—11:9

6. Shem and his descendants 11:10-26

National Beginnings:
   7. Abraham and his family 11:27—25:11
   8. Ishmael and his descendants 25:12-18
   9. Isaac and his family 25:19—37:1
  10. Jacob and his family 37:2—50:26
In 1 Corinthians it is evident that Paul was answering questions or addressing problems that had been communicated to him from Corinth. Paul deals with one question at a time. After addressing the large problem of unity in the church (1:1—4:21), he raises the question of two problems that were rumored about Corinth (chapters 5 and 6), and then the letter deals with each additional problem by beginning, "Now concerning . . ." So the sections of the letter are easily divided at 7:1 ("Now concerning the matters about which you wrote . . ."), 8:1 ("Now concerning food offered to idols . . ."), 12:1 ("Now concerning spiritual gifts . . ."), 15:1 ("Now I would remind you . . ."), and 16:1 ("Now concerning the contribution . . .").

However you arrive at an outline, whether by dividing the book up into paragraphs, or by borrowing someone else's out-line—the point is now to give attention to smaller units of the book. The outline should be a broad one with major headings, not a detailed analytical outline. If the outline you have bor-rowed is broken down into second and third subheadings, then discard that part of the outline and give attention only to the major headings.

Second Reading—Outline
Now read each section of the book. After each heading in your notebook, write a summary of what you have read. What is the main thought in the section? How was it illustrated? What was the major historical action? Describe what you have read in one easily recoverable paragraph.

At the end of the book, you should be able to read your informal summaries and recall the basic message of the book step by step. By now you have gone from a broad reading of the whole book down to a more careful reading of the book by separate major headings. The third reading, as I will show, takes us a step further in the *analysis* of the text, after we have taken steps to prepare the way.

Preparation for Third Reading

The object of this method of Bible study is firsthand experience of the Bible. I have avoided, for that reason, too much reliance on helps of various kinds outside of the Bible itself. It has been a serious weakness of all kinds of attempts to study the Bible that students are led off into reading *about* the Bible and neglect an actual reading of the books themselves.

But there comes a time when commentaries, Bible dictionaries, Bible encyclopedias and the like are more than helpful—they are indispensable. By encouraging a firsthand reading, I do not intend to discourage availing ourselves of the accumulated knowledge and wisdom concerning the Bible. Both archeology and textual studies have shed a floodlight on biblical study and have given us insights that we could scarcely acquire on our own, even over a lifetime. Further, there has been a 2,000-year-plus tradition of biblical exegesis that has yielded a many-faceted treasury of Bible interpretation. We put ourselves in the stream of these powerful currents of Bible knowledge when we lay hold of the better products of biblical study.

Find at least one article in a Bible dictionary or Bible encyclopedia that gives an introduction to the book itself. Commentaries will also have an introductory article, giving pertinent background information for the study of each book.

At the end of this chapter I have listed a few of the better resources for reasonably brief articles on Bible subjects. The list is by no means exhaustive, but it suggests some of the more readily available good, readable, reference works for Bible study.

As you read one, two or three general articles on the book in question, keep notes in your notebook. Organize your findings under headings such as these:

1. Authorship
2. Historical period
3. Occasion for the composition of this book

4. Major themes
5. Minor themes
6. Related modern studies of this book (usually listed in a bibliography at the end of dictionary articles)
7. Relevant geographical facts

These brief articles constitute only the beginning of study into the secondary works on books of the Bible. Very likely you could never get to the end of reading all the volumes written on the single book of Romans. But these secondary works lead us to an understanding of the historical background, geographical background and the language of a text in such a way that the book begins to take on a new depth. Isaiah's prophecy of Immanuel takes on new immediacy when we realize the danger posed by Syria's and Israel's pact against Judah in those days. Paul's career at Ephesus and his letter to the churches in that area from prison have new meaning for us when we discover that seacoast town as a center of depraved religion and disordered life—or when it dawns on us that Paul spent at least two years of obscure labor in that sin-infested crossroads of Europe and Asia.

The Revelation cannot fail to impress us with the seriousness of Christian discipleship in the first century when we see it against the background of Domitian's persecution, or in light of the history of the emperor Nero's devastation of the church three decades earlier. Early martyrdom, once the dimensions and reality of this bloodletting of Christians in the first century is realized, causes the innocent phrases of 1 Peter suddenly to come alive and burn with the passions of a life devoted to crossbearing. Knowing the background of the prison epistles evokes in us those sympathies so necessary for understanding why Paul believed the rewards of eternity far outweighed the considerable costs of Christian discipleship.

In every way, historical, biographical and geographical backgrounds prepare us to read the words with new eyes. References that appeared, at first sight, of no great importance, suddenly appear pregnant with meaning, full of associations that we could hardly have realized at our first reading.

Third Reading—Analysis

Fortified by two readings of the book, a progressively closer look at the text, and a knowledge of the book's historical and interpretive background, you are now ready for an even closer, analytical reading. The purpose this time is to take each of the major headings, or each paragraph, and discover as much about the content of that section as possible.

A time-honored reporting method, and one that is useful to us here, is to ask five basic questions: the five *W*'s—Who? What? Why? When? Where?

Let's take a sample Scripture paragraph and see how this might work. Matthew 26:36-46:

Then Jesus went with them to a place called Gethsemane, and he said to his disciples, "Sit here, while I go yonder and pray." And taking with him Peter and the two sons of Zebedee, he began to be sorrowful and troubled. Then he said to them, "My soul is very sorrowful, even to death; remain here, and watch with me." And going a little farther he fell on his face and prayed, "My Father, if it be possible, let this cup pass from me; nevertheless, not as I will, but as thou wilt." And he came to the disciples and found them sleeping; and he said to Peter, "So, could you not watch with me one hour? Watch and pray that you may not enter into temptation; the spirit indeed is willing, but the flesh is weak." Again, for the second time, he went away and prayed, "My Father, if this cannot pass unless I drink it, thy will be done." And again he came and found them sleeping, for their eyes were heavy. So, leaving them again, he went away and prayed for the third time, saying the same words. Then he came to the disciples and said to them, "Are you still sleeping and taking your rest? Behold, the hour is at hand, and the Son of man is betrayed into the hands of sinners. Rise, let us be going; see, my betrayer is at hand."

Asking the five basic reporting questions helps us to focus closely on certain aspects of the passage, but from different points of view. So it is often surprising to see how the Scripture opens up to us during this process. Begin with the first question.

WHO? The main figures come into focus here. There was Jesus, of course, but who was with him? Peter, James and John. Our memory may tell us already that these were major figures among the Apostles. They were with Jesus at the Mount of Transfiguration, and when Jesus gave that great teaching on the Mount of Olives concerning his second coming. Every list of Apostles in the Gospels begins with these three, and they figure prominently in every account, especially in the first three Gospels.

Looking up the name of any one of these in a Bible dictionary will confirm what we have already guessed—that these three constitute an inner circle of Jesus' disciples. They probably came out of the following of John the Baptist, and they were among the first to follow Jesus in Galilee.

The one who is centrally addressed in this passage is the one whom Jesus called "My Father." There is more than a touch of pathos in this. Jesus had all along been calling on God as "Abba"—the intimate family name for father in Aramaic. Now it was that very relationship of Father and Son that was at stake. In Jesus' eyes, obedience alone—even obedience to the death—established that he was the Son and that God could be known as Father. He taught his disciples to pray to God as Father, but even their relationship as children of God depended on Jesus' claim to be the Son. On the other hand, in the eyes of the world and even of his disciples, Jesus' death on the cross would eliminate every claim to Sonship. The prayer is addressed to Father—faithful and loving—but the subject is the abandonment of the Son.

And then there is one other figure, only in the shadows of this passage, but he is significant. Jesus mentions "my betrayer." Evil intention disguised as friendship: that is the point here.

Answering to the *Who?* in your analysis of a passage lets you focus closely on persons you may easily miss in a more hurried reading. And it helps to bring out characteristics in the main figures that may not always be seen in other passages. Try to draw as many lines of thought, fact and relationship to these characters as possible. You can be helped in this by making a simple chart. Divide a sheet of paper in your notebook into three columns, heading each column with (1) Who? (2) Comments and Observations, and (3) Further Study (see figure 1).

Mark 1:40-45

<u>Who?</u>   <u>Comments & Observations</u>   <u>Further Study</u>
leper   begs;   How were
         seems confident   lepers treated
         of Jesus' ability   in Jewish
         yet questions   society?
         his willingness   What does
         to heal   the law say?

Figure 1. Sample Study Chart

In the first column you need simply the name. In the second column let your thoughts flow, writing what you already know about this figure, what you observe in the passage, what you might discover through research, further questions and even speculation. These comments are to be experimental, not the finished product of careful research, but something that helps you to think through (*imagine* through) and flesh out the people in the passage. Then, in the third column write a short note on those matters you want to research further with the use of Bible dictionaries, encyclopedias, commentaries and so forth. You can do this sort of extra research as you go along or wait and catch up at the end of the book study.

After *Who?* comes *What? Why? When?* and *Where?* all using a similar procedure with three columned pages or sections of pages. In some books one of these questions will stand out more than the others. In the Gospels, for instance, it will likely be the *Who? When?* and *Where?* that are significant. In the letters of Paul, I would expect the *What?* and *Why?* to be more important in the lengthier sections.

The real test of these methods in any book, however, is patient and persistent application. Here is the true heart of Bible study. As we learn to study the books of the Bible, we learn the secret of the Bible itself.

Further Helps for Bible Study
I. Bible Dictionaries and Encyclopedias
1. *The Interpreter's Dictionary of the Bible.* Ed. George A. Buttrick. Nashville: Abingdon Press, 1962.

Here is a complete four-volume dictionary with a one-volume supplement (general editor, Keith Crim, 1976) composed of articles by some of the best scholars on both sides of the Atlantic, the authors reflecting a wide range of theological views. Each article ends with a brief bibliography that will especially help those who want to dig deeper.
2. *The New Bible Dictionary.* Ed. J. D. Douglas. Grand Rapids: Wm. B. Eerdmans Publishing Co., 1975.

Editors for this one-volume dictionary include such luminaries as F. F. Bruce and J. I. Packer. In many ways it sets the standard for clear, concise, and illuminating articles reflecting a consistent evangelical point of view.
3. *Harper's Encyclopedia of Bible Life.* Madeleine A. and J. Lane Miller, revised by Boyse M. Bennett, Jr., and David H. Scott. New York: Harper & Row, 1978.

This volume comments on the Bible by providing a backdrop of everyday affairs which are often alluded to, but hardly ever explained, in the biblical text itself. Homes, food, clothing, medicine, feasts, the life of nomads, farmers and artisans are topics that suggest the general design of this quite helpful reference work.
II. One-Volume Commentaries
1. *The Interpreter's One-Volume Commentary on the Bible.* Ed. Charles M. Laymon. Nashville: Abingdon Press, 1971.

This provides a very concise, somewhat technical commentary on each book of the Old and New Testaments and the Apocrypha. Again a wide range of theological views are included. One of the best features of this volume is a chronological table and article on chronology by Gordon B. Duncan in the appendices.

2. *The New Bible Commentary: Revised.* Ed. Donald Guthrie, Alec Motyer, Alan Stibbs and Donald Wiseman. Grand Rapids: Wm. B. Eerdmans Publishing Co., 1970.

Some of the most helpful general articles and historical tables will be found in this one-volume collection. The commentary on each biblical book (it does not include the Apocrypha) highlights biblical themes and the biblical writer's intentions without being too preoccupied with problems of authorship and date. It is especially helpful in its attention to significant Hebrew and Greek words that play pivotal roles in the interpretation of the text. Again all the contributors reflect an evangelical point of view.

3. *Peake's Commentary on the Bible.* Ed. Matthew Black and H. H. Rowley. Nashville: Thomas Nelson and Sons Ltd., 1976.

Long one of the most valued of one-volume commentaries, it calls to mind the recent tradition of British Bible scholars with names such as Wheeler Robinson, James Moffatt and C. F. D. Moule.

the sort of study known as typology—finding types that prefigure important events and people within the text—and we have enough to keep several medieval scholars busy for a lifetime.

But, gratefully, there are other more productive ways of looking at the Bible. At least part of studying the Bible, however, involves using all sorts of devices—artificial though they may sometimes be, and limited as they almost always are—in order to dig beneath the surface of Scripture and see what is there.

It is really a matter of allowing the imagination to come into play, viewing the Scripture from different perspectives. On the one hand we might look at Scripture from the point of view provided by biography. David himself illuminates 1 and 2 Samuel. A study of Peter in Mark and Acts will give a vision of those books that a less focused study will not.

On the other hand, a topical study yields a rather different view of things. Years ago I wanted to do a study on the political references in the Gospels. Because of that study, which consisted simply of going through the Gospels and listing all the verses that had any relevance to politics, I discovered firsthand how much more the Gospel of Matthew concentrates on kingship and the kingdom of heaven than any of the other Gospels.

In the following pages I want to suggest a few ways you can add variety to the ways you read. There are at least a dozen books today that deal almost exclusively, and sometimes exhaustively, with this particular topic: namely, variety in approaches to Bible study. I have no desire to duplicate what has already been given in that area. One book that I have in hand lists and describes twelve ways of Bible study—from devotional study to word study to a study of individual verses to a study of the book's background. These can certainly be helpful.

What I want to describe here are a few methods that seem to be most fruitful in terms of looking at Scripture from various perspectives, and then to see these as a *supplement* to the more basic study of the Bible. But these are not a supplement in the sense of only being additional items that are hardly necessary or barely worthy of consideration. These are necessary in that they lay open and stir up some streams of biblical truth that may otherwise be overlooked. They cannot replace a solid study of individual books, but without a variety of methods many facets of Scripture will fail to make an impression on our minds.

The following seven methods are intended to cut through Scripture at decisive points and increase the opportunity to bring a lively imagination into play in Scripture study.

I. The Topical Method

This method is a straightforward method of digging out passages relating to a particular topic. Any topic will be treated in a similar way, of course, and the subjects are endless—from Angels to Love to Zion.

Resources
☐ A Bible
☐ An exhaustive concordance
☐ A Bible dictionary or encyclopedia

Suggestions
1. *Define your topic carefully.* The more narrowly you define your topic the more manageable your study will be. If the topic is God, then you might never get through. But if the topic is an attribute of God, such as God's power or God's love, it becomes more manageable. But even better is to break one of these topics up into manageable subtopics and deal with them one at a time. For instance:
God's Love
1. God's love of the world
2. God's love of Israel
3. God's love of the Son
4. God's love of the gentile nations
5. God's long-suffering love
6. God's covenant love
7. God's love of an individual
2. *Consult a Bible dictionary or encyclopedia.* This will give you (1) an idea of some general conclusions in this area of study and (2) some of the major texts that deal with this topic.

3. *Make a list of synonyms and related words, and keep this list at the beginning of your notes.* If your topic were God's covenant love, then you would want to be alert to such key words as *covenant, chosen, elected, conceived, fellowship, covenant people—my people, Israel's God, love, compassion, mercy, sympathy, loving-kindness, lover, friend, father—child.*

4. *Carefully define the scope of your research.* A topic such as the kingdom of God can be the subject of a search through the entire Old and New Testaments, but limiting the scope of the study is a better strategy. By carefully researching the topic in an encyclopedia you will arrive at those areas of the Bible that would yield the greatest results. "The kingdom of God" or, alternately, "the kingdom of heaven" is mentioned most prominently and explicitly in the Gospels of Matthew, Mark and Luke. Confining your study, at least in its first stage, to these books will get at the heart of the matter. Then, at a later stage, the sources of the kingdom idea can be explored in Judges, Samuel, Kings and other places.

The principle: Use your research tools to suggest how the scope of your work should proceed from the most important books to those of lesser importance for that topic.

5. *Use an exhaustive concordance to locate passages that relate specifically to your topic.* This will help you discover some of the most important passages, but don't trust this approach alone. Only those passages that expressly mention a key word in your topic can be found by this method.

6. *List all passages that relate to your topic.* Write out the briefer passages. Summarize the longer ones.

7. *Make a list of the personal conclusions you draw from each stage of the study.* These conclusions can be grouped in such categories as (1) historical (facts relating to background, persons, events), (2) doctrinal (teachings on various issues), (3) devotional, and (4) ethical.

II. Biographical Method
In a very important sense biography—the story of a life—is what Scripture centrally reveals. What Scripture discloses is not

a description of God but a description of people who themselves have had an experience of God. In observing these individual lives, with their varied gifts, struggles, sins, triumphs
and joys, we begin to find our own way to God. Abraham Heschel's words that the Bible is not "man's theology, but God's
anthropology" are right to the point in appreciating the importance of this kind of study.

No other focus on a single facet of Bible study can be more
fruitful than this one.

Resources
☐ A Bible
☐ An exhaustive concordance
☐ A Bible dictionary or encyclopedia

Suggestions
1. *Be realistic about the length of time you want to spend on one
biographical study.* If you are investigating a person who appears
as a major character—Abraham, Moses, David, Paul and others
of that rank—you may find that the project is considerably
more than you bargained for in terms of time needed to complete the study. A figure who did not occupy the limelight quite
as much can prove to be a real treasury of insight into Scripture.
Isaac, Lot, Aaron, Caleb, Deborah, Ruth, Amos, Baruch, Zerubbabel, Matthew, Mary Magdalene, Martha of Bethany, Silas,
John Mark, Priscilla and Aquila—these are only a few of the
lives which, in a relatively short study, will yield priceless results
in biblical insight.
2. *Locate the principal books and passages that relate to the person
you intend to study.* The simplest way to do this, of course, is to
consult a Bible dictionary or encyclopedia where the main facts
and references are condensed into one article. A concordance
will locate the other passages that relate to your subject.
3. *List passages and summarize findings.*
4. *Write out conclusions concerning the life, actions, personality,
affections, strengths and weaknesses of your biographical subject.* Be
highly imaginative, even speculative in doing this. You are in-

terested in getting a feel for who this person is, why he or she believes or doesn't believe, what makes this person tick. What are his or her typical actions or reactions to events? How do people relate to this character? What adjectives describe your subject? Awe-inspiring or comfortable? Sociable or aloof? Intelligent or superficial? A person of strength and character, or fickle and indecisive? Go beyond the mere facts and press to gain a real insight into who this person is, how he or she has changed, and what circumstances have brought about this change.

III. The Word-Study Method
A biblical word study is both profitable and tricky. It is profitable in that concepts—even the most prominent theological concepts—often revolve around the definition, usage and history of a word. The word *promise,* for instance, can be traced through the Old and New Testaments revealing an intriguing pattern of added subtleties in the meaning of the word.

On the other hand, a word study is tricky because the words we use in a translation often do not correspond directly to the words that appear in the original language. *Love* appears in Hebrew in several forms, most of which are taken from the metaphor meaning "to breathe after" or "to long for." In Greek there are four distinct words, each corresponding to a different kind of love—romantic love, friendship, affection, and sacrificial love or divine love. There are five words—*phos, phengos, phoster, lychnos,* and *lampas*—all translated by the one English word "light." "Time" is translated from two words, *chronos* and *kairos;* the former expressing the continuity of time, while the latter expresses a quality of time. The words in Greek for "people" correspond to English words like "ethnic groups," "tribes," "the citizens" and "the multitude"—but they do not correspond exactly and are used in ways that are not customary in English.

Viewed from another direction, several Greek terms are translated by more than one English word—and that depending on the context. For example, *koinonia* is sometimes "community," sometimes "fellowship" and sometimes "communion."

These facts should not deter us from a word study based on an English word. Even though there may be more than one word for *man,* we still have the concept of man as the real object of the study—no matter how many words, English and Greek or Hebrew, serve to express that concept. It should be borne in mind, however, that we are not dealing with the original language if we are studying an English Bible, and there are shades of meaning that simply will not come through without a study of Greek and Hebrew.

Short of study of the original languages, however, there are some worthwhile steps you can take to find new avenues of biblical study.

Resources
☐ Several translations of the Bible for comparison of words and phrases
☐ An exhaustive concordance
☐ A Bible dictionary or encyclopedia
☐ A word study such as A. T. Robertson's *Word Pictures in the New Testament* (Nashville: Broadman, 1943)

Suggestions
1. *Select a word.*
2. *Determine the scope of your study*—Old Testament, New Testament, the Gospels, the letters of Paul or some other unit of study.
3. If you have a set of word-study reference books, such as the one suggested above, *find several examples of the word you are making the object of your study and read the comments on the use of that word.*
4. *Use the exhaustive concordance to locate each instance your word appears in Scripture.* The use of a complete concordance, such as *Strong's Exhaustive Concordance of the Bible* (Nashville: Abingdon, 1980), can also shed light on the original Hebrew or Greek from which the word is translated. *Strong's* includes a Hebrew and Greek lexicon which is numerically keyed to the words of the main concordance.

If you are making a survey of the word *bless,* for instance, the entry is followed by number *1288* which locates the word in the Hebrew lexicon. The precise word in each passage is then traced to the word from which it was translated. Thus *bless* in Psalm 5:12 was translated from *barak* whose root meaning is "to kneel." This type of study can be of benefit even to those not acquainted with the original language.

5. *After you have surveyed each book, write down your conclusions concerning (1) the significance of the word, (2) the various uses of the word, (3) the changes in the use of the word from one part of Scripture to another, and (4) a definition of the word as it is used biblically.*

IV. A Study of Bible Themes

The study of a biblical theme is different from the study of a topic or a word. A theme is more than a subject; it must be expressed as a complete statement. "Only God can give real peace"—that is a theme. *Peace* can be the object of a topical study or of a word study. But in a thematic study you are looking for a particular point of view, an angle on peace. "The obedience required of a Christian," "the gifts of the Spirit," "the goal of redemption," "the meaning of worship"—all of these are topical. But "The result of obedience is freedom" is a thematic statement. So also is "Spiritual gifts contribute to unity," or "Our greatest longing is for God himself," or "Repentance is required for redemption."

A theme is, of course, narrower and more closely defined than a topic or a word study. It requires some preparation to locate that part of Scripture that would be most relevant to the theme you undertake to study. But a surprisingly small amount of preparation will lead to an enormously helpful study.

Resources
☐ A Bible
☐ A Bible dictionary or encyclopedia
☐ An exhaustive concordance
☐ One or more books of theology or Bible commentary that tells something about your theme

Suggestions

1. *Define your topic carefully.* Often thematic study may grow out of an effort to investigate something that came to light in outside reading. I have a book, for instance, that makes the point that "salvation results in freedom from sin." This can become my theme. First I find out which books and passages are important to the writer who articulated this theme in the first place. He might have relied primarily on Isaiah and John. So these two books would be among those in which I would investigate the theme.

2. *Determine which are the key words in the theme.*

3. *Consult a Bible dictionary or encyclopedia, referring to the key words in order to locate those passages that might relate to the theme.*

4. *Consult a concordance, again locating the key words in order to find possible areas where the theme is treated.*

5. *After these initial steps, determine which books or passages would be of greatest benefit in the study of this theme.*

6. *Read the books and passages.* Keep notes on relevant points made concerning the theme.

7. *Take note also of those scriptural positions that seem to run contrary to a theme.* It would hardly be a well-balanced study of "Obedience results in rewards from God"—a study that would certainly include Deuteronomy and Proverbs, two books that teach this theme very clearly—if it did not also include Job, which brings that basic teaching into question.

V. The Short Passage Study

This should be one of the most frequently used—and one of the most useful—forms of Bible study. The point is to take an appropriate unit of Scripture and do an intensive study.

How should you choose such a unit? It could be a chapter or a psalm, but it need not be. In many cases the chapter does not really indicate the true unit of thought. However, paragraphs do, although here, too, translators are often responsible for where paragraph divisions are made.

You might choose one paragraph or several paragraphs linked together. Sometimes it is helpful to focus on a passage

that is well known, but which you have not examined closely.
Some of the classic texts make for an especially rich Bible study.
Quite a number will sooner or later come to mind, but here are
a few that will always prove to be valuable studies:

OLD TESTAMENT

Genesis 1:1—2:4	1 Kings 3:3-28
Genesis 15:1-6	1 Kings 18:7-40
Genesis 17	Job 19
Exodus 20:1-17	Psalm 19
Exodus 33:12-23	Psalm 22
Deuteronomy 30	Psalm 23
Joshua 24	Psalm 100
1 Samuel 2:1-10	Isaiah 52:13—53:12
2 Samuel 12:1-15	Jeremiah 31:27-34

NEW TESTAMENT

Matthew 5:1—7:29	Ephesians 5:21—6:9
John 1:1-18	Philippians 2:1-18
Acts 9:1-22	1 Thessalonians 4:13—5:11
Romans 8	1 Peter 1:13-25
1 Corinthians 13	Revelation 21:1—22:5

In addition to these, at least four books can be treated as short
passages: Philemon, 2 and 3 John, and Jude.

This list can be expanded indefinitely, and you will quickly
find other passages (especially in the course of book studies)
that you will want to pursue in the manner described below.

Resources
☐ A Bible
☐ An alternate translation of the Bible
☐ An exhaustive concordance
☐ A Gospel parallel

Suggestions
1. *Select a short passage (1-3 paragraphs or so).*

2. *Read and then write a brief informal summary of the passage.*

3. *Compare the passage with the same passage in another translation.*

4. *If it is from one of the synoptic Gospels, compare the passage with the other two Gospels.* This can be done most easily, of course, if you use a Gospel parallel or harmony.

5. *List the major points that are made in the passage.* Under each of these points, list the supporting statements.

6. *Cross-refer your passage with others in the New Testament and Old Testament that relate to the main idea.* First, cross-refer from those books that are written by the same author. For instance, a passage from Romans can be illuminated by similar thoughts from other Pauline letters such as Ephesians and 1 Thessalonians. Second, cross-refer with books out of the same testament—Old Testament with Old Testament, and New Testament with New Testament. Third, find cross-references out of the other testament.

7. *Write out the personal application of this passage.* What difference might this Scripture make in the way you think, the way you perceive the world around you, the decisions you make or the actions you take?

VI. The Query Method

It is the most natural thing in the world—and I see it all the time—for people to go to Scripture with a question they want answered. That, more often than we imagine, is the very reason people get into Scripture in the first place. And at the point of facing that burning personal question, sometimes the most intense and interesting study takes place.

The query method should begin with a well-directed question:

☐ Why do good people suffer?

☐ How does one come to salvation?

☐ What did Jesus say about his second coming?

☐ Do signs announce the presence of the Holy Spirit?

☐ How did repentance, in Luke and Acts, relate to baptism and the gift of the Holy Spirit?

☐ Was Paul a zealot before his conversion?

The query method involves precisely the same procedure, using the same resources, as the theme method. The only difference is that you begin by formulating that vital question with which you wish to address Scripture. In the theme method, the idea or answer is already worked out—and you are looking for refinement and further insight. In the query method, the object of the study stands as a question mark, and you search for a way to get at the answer. With the theme method, the end of the journey is already well in mind, and you look for a roadmap to show you the way to get there. With the query method you know there must be a destination that answers your need, but first you must find its location. So, although the two *methods* are close to the same, their *intentions* are quite diverse.

VII. The Verse-by-Verse Study

On occasion you will want to focus closely on one verse. Or you will need to examine a significant passage in a step-by-step, verse-by-verse fashion. The following method will help you organize an approach to the study of one verse.

Resources
☐ A study Bible with cross-reference notes
☐ An exhaustive concordance
☐ A Bible dictionary or encyclopedia

Suggestions
1. *Begin by reading the verse several times and then writing a paraphrase of it.*
2. *List several responses to the verse.* What is your immediate reaction to the words and the meaning of the verse? What does it teach? What does it command? What are the implications of the thought contained in that verse?
3. *Use the study Bible to find other verses and passages that relate to the one you have selected.* List these in your notebook.
4. *Comment on the cross-reference verses.* What light is shed on the original verse by these cross-references? Write a brief state-

ment showing how the other passages illuminate the truth contained in the verse under examination.

5. *Use a Bible dictionary to examine significant words and names.* Suppose you were doing a study of Ephesians 4:30, "Do not grieve the Holy Spirit of God, in whom you were sealed for the day of redemption." You would profit from the use of a Bible dictionary to throw light on the words *Holy Spirit, seal* and *redemption.*

6. *List personal applications.* How does this verse apply to your own life? Does it make a difference in your thinking? An attitude? Does it call for a specific action? Write as many points—each very briefly—as occur to you.

None of these methods, in and of themselves, is sufficient for a well-balanced or comprehensive Bible study. None of them, by themselves, will result in an adequate program of study or a well-developed knowledge of the Bible. However, each of these methods can provide a unique insight into Scripture and a valuable supplement to a more comprehensive study. In addition to these are methods of study aimed specifically at devotion. This aim in Bible study is so important and so central to the very meaning of what we are doing, however, that I must take up the subject of devotional Bible study in a separate chapter.

PART III

Bible Reading in Home and Church

Principles and methods are not the end nor the goal of Bible study. Bible study is meant to transform our lives, and it should take place within three contexts (the last two of which have often been neglected): (1) personal devotions, (2) family and church, and (3) Christian mission into the world. Within these three contexts, each one influencing the other two, the grammar of faith becomes a living language.

9
Your Devotional Life: The Heart of Bible Study

The devotional study of the Bible is not another, optional method of study. It is the essential purpose of all Bible study. The Bible *is* a devotional book. It has emerged from intense experiences of God, from prolonged reflection on God, and it yields its inner meaning only to that same spirit and purpose.

Early in the life of the church, an allegorical method of interpreting Scripture gained wide acceptance, especially in the Western church. Some opposed this method of finding inner, secret meaning to Scripture even then; the Reformers of a later time—especially Luther and Calvin—firmly rejected it. The real meaning of Scripture should be strongly anchored, they believed, in the original historical and literal intention of Scripture. Luther went so far as to say, for instance, that Origen's allegories of Scripture "were not worth so much dirt," and that the method as a whole was a "sort of beautiful harlot who proves herself spiritually seductive to idle men."[1]

But in spite of all of the bricks, modern and medieval, that have been tossed at allegory and in spite of abuses that evidently have taken place, we must ask what insight into Scripture made this method of interpretation so appealing for so long. What purpose was being served? What intuitive element in the human soul responded to these fanciful interpretations?

I have not noticed any great movement back to the allegories of Origen and Augustine. And most, by far, of the expositors today favor the methods that give insight into the history and language of a passage and then uncover its original intention. Most interpreters today would tend to agree with Chrysostom— a fourth-century critic of the allegorical method—when he said that it is not right "to inquire curiously into all things in parables word by word, but when we have learnt the object for which it was composed, to reap this, and not to busy one's self about anything further."[2]

But this same Chrysostom, critical as he might have been of his contemporaries who found allegories everywhere in Scripture, did not entirely reject the method as can be seen by his allegorical interpretation of the parable of the wise and foolish virgins only a few pages after his comment denying the virtue of allegory. Why did even he find the lure of an inner, spiritual meaning too hard to resist at times? Why indeed did New Testament writers read into Old Testament prophecy and psalms ideas that likely never occurred to the original writers? Why, in fact, do we often find that Scripture speaks directly to our own circumstance, irrespective of its original context? The real question is, How and why do these ancient writings become a devotional text—a way of opening up avenues into the world and into the soul that does not diminish with time or distance, that is not subject to culture and geography, and that tempts all serious readers to draw conclusions about their own lives, their own times, and their own purpose no matter how far removed these are from the world of Aramean nomads, oriental kings and ancient itinerant teachers?

Three observations—about the nature of the book, the nature of those who read the book, and the situation that exists when the two are brought together—suggest why Scripture has proved so useful in the enrichment of the inner meditative and devotional life.

The Nature of the Bible

Many of the church fathers insisted that the Bible has more than one level of meaning. That is part of the answer as to why they were so attracted to the allegorical interpretation of Scripture. Origen, for example, said that just as man is comprised of body, soul and spirit, so Scripture has a body (its literal meaning), a soul (its moral meaning) and a spirit (its allegorical or spiritual meaning). Thus in the parable of the lost coin, the coin has an obvious literal meaning (it is a coin), it has a moral meaning (it is that for which we long and after which we seek), and it has a spiritual meaning (the kingdom of God).

What might be extracted from this idea need not be a full-blown defense of allegory. It might be an idea, a sentiment or a feeling that has endured even though allegorical preaching has long been abandoned. It was there the very first time someone saw in Paul's letter to the Corinthians something that could be addressed to other Corinths, other churches, even to other times. It was an unstated assumption when the Christian canon was formulated that these writings, aimed at specific audiences (sometimes just to one person, as in Philemon), bear within them a living principle, a spirit or an abiding sentiment that can once again be set loose and work its power within a new setting. Scripture is Scripture because it is found to have this virtue. From a human perspective, if it did not have that power, there would be no reason to include it in a canon preserved for posterity.

So the allegorical method was one way—an often unsatisfactory and rather artificial way in most instances—to adapt Scripture to differing circumstances and then to unleash its power into the life of the hearer. That, after all, is the purpose of all preaching and Bible reading. Without that hope and confidence, there is nothing left to sustain our interest in Scripture except an antiquarian curiosity. People come to Scripture not just to learn about Moses or Ezekiel, Mary or Paul, but to know how they themselves can live and think and see things in a new way. That is the real purpose of Scripture, without which all other purposes become trivial and futile.

The Nature of the Bible Reader
The second observation comes from the other direction. I have said that the Bible is *essentially* a devotional book. It is also a book of ethics, history and various types of literature. But the quality that permeates all of this and lifts it up to a new level of potency is that when we attend to this book it becomes for us *more* than ethics, *more* than history and *more* than literature.

Heinrich Heine said that the Bible is "the drama of the human race."[3] When he said this, of course, he did not mean it in the narrow sense that it is world history written on a smaller scale, although there might be some sense to that idea. Nor did he mean only that it is the "drama of redemption" as people often refer to the biblical account of God's mighty acts in history, even though there is something to that as well. What he meant was that in the Bible lies the full range of human possibilities, both good and evil, from the highest to the lowest. The dramatic conflict is seen at its most intense level. The human virtues of love, loyalty, courage, hope and faithfulness are found in degrees and forms that answer to the true variety of human experience. The suffering, the passions and the joys of human existence take on flesh and are known to us in the lives of Samuel, David, and Elisha, of Mary Magdalene and Paul of Tarsus.

Here is life—human life. The point of our greatest concentration is here. And anyone who reads these pages is always drawn by the contemplation of the divine, mirrored in human experience. Here we can most profitably reflect on life. Here we find ourselves and can see ourselves in our truest light. In the Bible are both the "alien dignity" of our being made in the image of God and the human pathology rooted in sin. In the Bible we find both our present predicament and our future destiny.

Bringing the Bible and Readers Together
But another question comes to the forefront now: Is it our true desire to reflect on these matters? However pure the truth presented and however salutary the effect, is there something with-

in us that draws us to these things? Do we, in fact, *want* worship and meditation and prayer?

The answer, I think, is both yes and no. A theology professor of mine once upbraided his class for not attending seminary chapel. "The problem is," he said, "we don't really want to worship." He was right, of course. There is something in us that avoids it like the plague. Any desire for quiet and reflection we suppress—partly because we are frightened by what we'll find there. We puncture the quiet with radios, busy ourselves with unneeded activities and court time-wasting entertainment because we fear boredom.

We need to be reminded that Paul, John and James all agreed on one point about sin: it begins with the ever ingenious suppression of the truth. And if we meditate on our lives long enough, in solitary quiet and with singular purpose, there is the ever present danger that the truth will dawn on us, and then we'll have to change. Reflection, meditation, worship can be costly. And such costs we are bound to resist.

On the other side, however, is the overwhelming reality of our desire for contemplation and worship. It is not only within Christian circles that this reality becomes explicit. Herman Melville, for instance, would hardly be placed in any particular orthodoxy, yet his writings lose most of their meaning if not seen within the irrepressible human longing to meditate until surface reality gives way to a deeper, inner truth. The whole of *Moby Dick* begins with this observation—even before Ishmael launches out upon the deep to meditate on the mysteries of the White Whale:

Circumambulate the city of a dreamy Sabbath afternoon. Go from Corlears Hook to Coenties Slip, and from thence, by Whitehall, northward. What do you see?—Posted like silent sentinels all around the town, stand thousands upon thousands of mortal men fixed in ocean reveries. . . . Tell me, does the magnetic virtue of the needles of the compasses of all those ships attract them thither? . . . Let the most absent-minded of men be plunged in his deepest reveries—stand that man on his legs, set his feet a-going, and he will infal-

libly lead you to water. . . . Yes, as every one knows, meditation and water are wedded for ever.[4]
This common observation becomes something more in the
hands of an Augustine of Hippo. What was so obvious to him
about human psychology—and about the suffering of the human psyche—is that human longing expresses itself in many
different ways. In everyday experience a man or woman longs
for material goods or for pleasure or recognition. But all of
these are inferior reflections of the great and very deep longing
that people have for God.

"We were made for thee, O God," Augustine said, "and our
hearts are restless until they find rest in thee." So the great
source of our problems as a race is not that we love things—
but that we love them more than they ought to be loved. We
give them the place in our hearts that must belong only to God.
Nevertheless, in spite of the disorder of our affections, the affections themselves—the great longing deep within each of
us—give abundant witness to the deep desire we have for God.
This longing, this propensity to contemplate God, is of the very
essence of human life.

The continual witness of those classic expressions of the
Christian life is that the nearer we draw to God the more we
experience of life. "I came that they may have life, and have
it abundantly" (Jn 10:10). A thirst for life is in reality a longing
for God, and those who expend their lives in devotion and
obedience to God are the ones who find life. Those, however,
whose affections are absorbed by things created by and inferior
to God are courting death. The search for heightened and
enlivened experience and the search for God are, if one would
rightly understand them, one and the same.

Thomas à Kempis expressed this matter when he said, "O
Light Eternal, transcending all created lights, cast Thy bright
beams from above, and penetrate the inmost recesses of my
heart. Cleanse, gladden, brighten, and enliven my spirit with all
its powers, that I may cleave to Thee with ecstasies of joy."[5]

Philipp Melanchthon, the great theologian of the German
reformation, had learned that the center of all desire in life is

God. Near death and still working, though his life's strength was ebbing away, he was asked if he wanted anything. "Nothing but heaven, so ask me nothing more."[6] These were his last words—a fitting summation of a life driven inexorably to that sublime conclusion.

But the Bible's continual message is always just that same point. When all choices are broken down to their essentials, only one real choice is made in life and that is whether to live or die. Sin, said Paul, means death. Disobedience, said Moses, means death. Death is the real meaning of every choice that denies the reality and lordship of God.

In Deuteronomy, the speech that Moses gave concerning the obligations of the law concluded with the solemn warning that Israel's obedience to the commandments was the path of life: "I call heaven and earth to witness against you this day, that I have set before you life and death, blessing and curse; therefore choose life" (Deut 30:19).

It should be no wonder, then, that our strongest desire is for life. Thus the contemplation of him who is the source of life is itself a vital fountain of living waters deep within us. In a contrary way, we also possess a propensity toward death, back to the dust and away from the life-giving Spirit: this cannot be denied and we see it in many forms. That is why the New Testament so often refers to the deep conflict between the flesh and the spirit—that which tends toward death and that which tends toward life. And it is the desire for life that is awakened and called forth by the study of Scripture.

The desire for life is often suppressed, diverted or dissipated. But it is there, and the powerful flow from those recesses deep within our souls continually exerts its pressure on our personalities, our thinking and our actions. Once in a while those great subterranean streams are tapped and stirred, at times by a word, an action, the sight of something or someone—things that touch us so deeply and call forth such undeniable responses that we hardly know how or why it happens. We simply know that something deep within us has been stirred, something that responds to truth and beauty and goodness. And when that happens, we often say that we have worshiped.

That is when we might respond as Edwin Hatch did when he wrote:

Breathe on me, Breath of God
 Till I am wholly Thine,
Till all this earthly part of me
 Glows with Thy fire divine.[7]

A Nonmethodical Approach to a Method

So how do we approach this important use of the Bible as a devotional book, as a touchstone of worship and meditation?

I am a firm believer that sometimes we need to be better acquainted with elementary practices in the Christian disciplines. Richard Foster's *Celebration of Discipline* has done much to remind us of the basic disciplines of meditation, fasting, prayer, solitude, service and so on. In prayer or meditation we are helped if some form is given to help us until our legs gain strength and we can walk on our own.

But when we come to using the Bible for the devotional life, I am somewhat reluctant to simply boil it down to a methodical approach. There are methods that one can use. Walter Trobisch wrote a short essay on Martin Luther's way of weaving Scripture into a four-strand garland.[8] I recommend that approach. I have used it and benefited from it. I have also asked several people, whose experience in these matters I trust, how they use Scripture in their devotional life. Here are some of their answers, which I have either elaborated or condensed a bit:

"I use a devotional book, like Oswald Chambers's My Utmost for His Highest. *This focuses closely on one meaningful, brief passage and then gives me commentary to set me thinking about the passage."*

"I read at random until I run across a passage that jumps off the page and speaks to my personal situation. Then I settle on those words and read them over and over again. I pray and let God say all that he wants to say to me through those words."

"I determine a program of reading. For instance, I might decide to read one chapter a day of Isaiah. That gets me ready for prayer, and

I let the words of that chapter suggest a subject or an image to meditate on. I think of that image—of a 'lamb,' or the 'suffering servant' who is bruised for our iniquities, or of the 'scarlet sins' being changed to the 'whiteness of snow.' And when nothing but that image or subject occupies the better part of my mind, I am ready to wait on God in prayer."

"I read from a list of suggested Bible readings that are designed to lead me through the Bible in one year. After the reading, my mind is settled, and I am ready for prayer."

"I go to the well-known and well-loved passages: Psalm 23, the Sermon on the Mount, the Lord's Prayer. I think there must be a reason that these have been so well loved through the years. I read the same passage day after day for a week. By the end of that week, many new things have occurred to me in prayer that I have never before seen in those passages."

"In the morning, or on the evening before, I write down a passage of Scripture to carry in my pocket. I try to memorize that passage during the day. This Scripture—sometimes one verse or two, sometimes much longer—becomes a focus for my prayer and meditation during the day. Even when I am driving to work, I can repeat the Scripture verses to myself, and that just naturally leads me into prayer."

"I divide a book up into thirty or thirty-one parts, reading one part a day. In this way I cover one book in a month. It is easy to do Proverbs this way since it has thirty-one chapters. Also the Psalms can be read, five psalms a day, in a month. Each of these 'parts' is brief enough to be read easily, and then, they become the Scripture that I meditate on. Sometimes I read them several times during the day."

"I read a passage. Then I focus on a sentence. Finally my thoughts play on the meanings and the sound of one essential word in that sentence. In this exercise, secrets are unlocked that a more cursory reading of Scripture can never encounter."

These are all good approaches. And there is room for quite a number of variations.

But what I want to stress here is that we are no more obliged to find a regimen of using Scripture in our devotional lives than we are to learn an approach for the sake of viewing a sunset. Melville saw how people were drawn to the water; there they found themselves in meditative reveries. He would not have dreamed of describing this phenomenon as if it were an exercise that people engaged in for the sake of their souls on a Sunday afternoon. No, they were drawn to the water by their own inner need and by the qualities of water.

But isn't it already obvious that men and women are drawn more to the Word than to water? Is there any need to say that when we read these words—however we read them, whether slowly and deliberately, memorizing verses, focusing on single words or devouring chapters and books at a time, whether methodically or randomly—we are drawn to meditate on the reality of God? Is there any need to channel that meditative spirit, restrict it to trained forms and heighten the expectation of rewards? Or is it enough to invite someone to see the glory and tragedy of human life—cast in the very image of God—and to wonder at what all this means?

There is something almost inevitable in what I am trying to describe concerning the devotional use of Scripture. If it is true that in this book are deep pools reflecting all that God has revealed concerning himself, if it is true that we long at the deepest levels of our souls for that very truth and that sentiment found in the Bible, if these matters accurately depict the correspondence between Bible readers and the Bible, then the devotional reading of Scripture can happen at any time we are drawn, or even disciplined, to sit down alone with the Book.

"Not without cause, and not without effect," said George Buttrick, "have men found in every age that prayer and Bible study are necessarily joined."[9] Deep calls unto deep. The One who inspired Scripture is the same One who meets the man or woman who prays. The truth of the written Word corresponds to the truth made known by the power and presence of the Holy Spirit. One draws on the other; one gives rise to the other; one confirms the other.

But, if it is not the method or the means or the approach that makes the difference, what does?

The question becomes sharper if we ask, Why is it that some can live all their lives with Scripture—reading it in a dutiful or perfunctory manner—and seemingly never be deeply affected by it? It is as if that performance were a necessary penance that would finally issue treasures in heaven. Or why can some become rather successful scholars, mastering the original language of the text, delving into questions of authorship, editing and the traditions that stand behind the text, and yet never seem to be gathering into their lives the warmth and vitality which so characterize the words they study? How do they live *with* the Word and not feel compelled to live *by* the Word?

That which *makes* Bible reading a devotional reading is more than a method, it is an attitude—even a certain passion—a willingness to go outside of ourselves in the discovery of that which is greater and infinitely more important than we are. It is a realization that we are confronted by a superior Word that renders all our lesser words as chaff driven before the wind. There is all the difference in the world between an approach to the text in which we sit as the judge, applying our critical faculties in study (a function which is nevertheless not to be denied!), and an approach which puts us figuratively or literally on our knees, willing to have our own lives judged by the searching light of God's Word. Buttrick, himself a great scholar, took note of this difference when he pointed out that "lowly saints unversed in knowledge about the scriptures are still found of God as they read, while 'Bible scholars' may grope through a deserted shrine."[10]

Augustine addressed the issue by asking, "What kind of spirit is required for the study of holy scripture?" His conclusion was that the most important quality is love.[11] Though it may seem odd to associate it with study, love is precisely what drives us out of our dark, self-confined quarters into the open light of God's truth. Love lets us be small and God's Word great; it allows us to find in the ancient passions of nations and men something of saving significance; it enables us to follow the paths of righteousness with a hunger and thirst for the reality of God.

With this spirit we can wander the fields and woods of Scripture and contemplate the wonders of God and the awesomeness of his work. In this spirit it matters not so much which

10
Bible Study
in the
Family

The most important experiences in our lives somehow show up in our language. That is nearly always so. Often I can tell whether a student has been studying accounting or data processing by the kind of vocabulary he uses in ordinary conversation—even when he is not speaking of those subjects. A biology major or a physics student is even easier to point out.

That is no extraordinary skill on my part. It is simply a common observation: People find that the vocabulary they pick up in even a narrow field of experience is also useful in describing and analyzing and communicating about the world around them.

I knew a church leader once who was quite interested in whether his staff members were "team players." He advised them to work out a "game plan" in order to "tackle" difficult problems. It should be no surprise to learn that in his college days he was a football player and a rather successful one. That was an important life experience for him, and the experience showed up in the way he communicated.

All of us do roughly the same thing. Our vocabulary—the way we communicate, or think, or relate to people—comes from significant experiences that we have had.

Why Families Need Bible Knowledge
Listen to a family speak.

Before long you can tell what is the center (or the centers) of its experience. If its language is filled with references to television programs, then a TV set is likely the altar of their common experience. In communication they allude to situation comedies, soap operas, even commercials. For those with an interest in athletics, sports serve as the core of their common experience. Their talk is filled with language that has the gridiron or the baseball diamond as a major point of reference. Even when they are not speaking about baseball, they clearly view the world from the pitcher's mound. And although sports-centered experience is less artificial and more a part of "real life" than televised fiction, it is still only a surface experience. There is no possibility of drawing on those lessons of life that enable people to order their existence in a meaningful way.

Even worse is the occasion when members of a family are not speaking a common language at all. The important experiences of the father are altogether different from those of the mother. And the parents are foreigners to the world of the young people who share the same address. Their language reflects the crisis in the family. They communicate poorly because their thinking (and thus their language) reflects diverse experiences in life. Historically, people living in close proximity who do not share the same language tend to live in conflict with or indifference toward each other. It is no different for the family. Whatever the outward result of the crisis, the family lacks communion—it lacks fellowship—because their means of communication has been weakened.

The Bible and Family Communication
The solution to this problem should be obvious—even if it is not easy to achieve. The family needs a common language. But more than that, it needs a language that is capable of communicating the most important ideas, the deepest feelings and the

strongest commitments that we humans experience.

The rules of baseball require a simple and straightforward level of communication. The plot of a soap opera requires slightly less sophistication in one's speech. But intimate human relationships require a subtlety and strength of communication. The covenant of marriage—as important as it is to the health of society—is hardly a self-evident concept. And the more a society's language becomes preoccupied with surface events and materialistic values, the more difficult it becomes to express the value and the dimensions of a deep personal commitment to another person. The deeper, and thus more human, experiences require a language and power of expression equal to the feelings and thoughts they convey.

The idea or the experience of love, for example, requires great subtlety and skill in order to give it proper expression. It remains a vague and elusive sentiment until it is given language equal to the subject matter. Only then is it possible to begin fleshing out its reality and measuring its dimensions. Through the Christian centuries, love has been made solid and understandable by the picture language we find in the Bible. In that book people found the shepherd who loved his lost lamb, the father who loved his prodigal son, the God whose love was made visible and historical in the Incarnation.

Love had always been there. But it had never been expressed quite that well before. And, in a sense, it had never been as real.

If you have followed the basic theme of this book—that Bible study provides the essential grammar and vocabulary of faith—then you should be aware that this is an especially important chapter. It is important because *it is within the family that we learn to speak.* We need to learn to speak of baseball and budgets, certainly, but we also need to speak of love and loyalty, of sadness, sympathy and joy.

Where personal relationships are first experienced and where they are experienced most intensely is also the place where we can learn a language that expresses intimacy and deep personal commitment. Language is never called to a higher task than that of expressing love, forgiveness, fairness, beauty, loyalty, sympathy and encouragement. In the family we learn what those words mean—and how to express them in a thousand different ways. Not all of our expressions (especially within the family) are explicit and verbal. But language—the words we use, the references we make, the common experiences we allude to—remains our most important means of knowing and communicating things important in personal relationships.

One principle is more evident in the family than in any other context, even though it is true in every situation; namely, all effective communication has its basis in common experience. Effective speakers appeal to an audience's experience, something that they will recognize as peculiarly their own and that they share in common. Every good public speaker is aware that his audience is mostly young or mostly aged, that his audience is made up of Italian New Yorkers, Irish midwesterners or rural Georgians.

In the family we instinctively appeal to those common experiences that are peculiarly our own—whether it is Aunt Martha's fetish of tidiness or Dad's habit of forgetting birthdays or little brother's unforgettable faux pas on a visit to the neighborhood socialite's house. Incidents, stories told and retold, become the stock from which we communicate.

So do television commercials.

So does gossip.

And so do the images, stories, poetry, characters and doctrine of the Bible.

So how can the Bible become the mother lode of the language we use within a family?

Marriage and the Word

A marriage is created by the word. It is a spoken promise—witnessed by the God who instituted marriage—that makes a married couple out of two distinct individuals.

If marriage is created by the spoken word, it is no wonder that the grammar of love, faith, loyalty and hope is so important to the strength and vitality of marriage.

No other relationship is so utterly dependent on the word.

Children have a certain biological and, for many years, material dependence on their parents. Employers have financial and legal obligations to employees and to their clientele. Friendships are formed in various ways, and they are often transient. But marriage, built as it is on what seems to be an ephemeral word, can be the strongest bond in all the many kinds of social attachments. And it is strong precisely to the degree that that spoken promise is seen to transcend every expediency ("for better, for worse; for richer, for poorer; in sickness and in health").

Bonhoeffer pointed out that it is marriage that sustains love, not love that sustains marriage. It is not a varying emotional state that forms the foundation of the family; it is the unalterable word.

This is why there is no relationship that more clearly needs the power of expression that the Bible affords than the marriage covenant. Everything that strengthens the initial words of promise and enriches the experience is a help to the marriage. The Bible—more than any other common source—can provide the deepest and most abiding expression of those qualities and virtues that constitute a healthy marriage. That is, first and foremost, because the Bible expresses the truth. "Are you leaving also?" Jesus asked his disciples. "Where shall we go?" they asked, "For you have the words of life." That which is grounded in truth has power to speak words of life to a marriage relationship. But the Bible is able to do this not only because it contains the truth, but because of the way it expresses the truth. It gives expression to those things that are the lifeblood of human relationships, including the most sacred of all human relationships, marriage.

Approaches to Bible Study for Married Couples

The simplest approach is probably the best. It is difficult for one person to incorporate a new endeavor into a schedule. For two people trying to do the same thing, plus trying to coordinate their efforts with each other, the task is not simply doubled, it is probably quadrupled. But it is well worth every effort for a married couple to make Bible study a shared experience. And there is more than one way the matter can be accomplished. Here are a few:

The Reading and Listening Exercise. One way is simply to set aside time on a daily basis to study Scripture together. Decide on a limited portion—one book or a series of psalms—that will become your joint project in Bible study. Then try the following procedure:

1. One person reads a chapter or a portion while the other listens. The one who listens is given the responsibility of writing down the theme or the main thought expressed in the passage.

2. The listener responds by reading his or her version of the passage's main thought.

3. Husband and wife discuss the theme and any aspect of the theme that may apply to their marriage, their work or their Christian growth.

4. The couple pray together for wisdom in applying this passage to life.

The Study-Report Method. Some couples may find it more to their liking to study separately and then to discuss the results of their study.

1. They should agree on a definite portion that they will study during the week together. From Monday through Friday they should each read and take notes on their reading.

2. Each day they would then give attention to (a) the main themes of their reading and (b) how that theme might apply to their own lives and their own world. Notes can be arranged in a stenographic pad in two columns as in figure 2.

3. On Saturday, at a prearranged, convenient time, the couple simply compare notes and discuss the similarities and contrasts of their discoveries in Scripture.

The Comparison Study Method. In the study-report method both the husband and wife must study the same portion of Scripture. The comparison study method provides an interesting variation in which husband and wife study different, but related, portions of Scripture.

This works best with reasonably small portions or books that

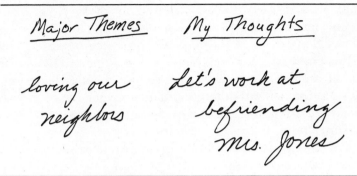

Major Themes   *My Thoughts*

loving our neighbors   *Let's work at befriending mrs. Jones*

Figure 2. Sample Study-Report

can be completed in a week's time. The following list gives examples of related passages that could be used:

Genesis 1—3 and Romans 1—2	Matthew and Luke
Psalm 19 and Proverbs 3	John and Matthew/Mark/or Luke
1 John and 1 Peter	Exodus 20 and Matthew 5
Ephesians and Colossians	Ezra and Nehemiah
1 and 2 Corinthians	1 Chronicles and 1 and 2 Samuel
1 and 2 Thessalonians	2 Chronicles and 1 and 2 Kings
1 Timothy and Titus	Job and Ecclesiastes
2 Peter and Jude	Amos and Hosea
Matthew and Mark	Isaiah 1—12 and Micah
Mark and Luke	

These are only a few of the possible combinations. The important consideration is that the selected portions have (1) a common topic, (2) a common author or (3) a common historical period.

Bible Study for Children
Coleridge, so the story of the great essayist goes, was visited by

a man who insisted that he believed in giving children no religious instruction until they were old enough to choose their own religious views. With great self-assurance he announced that his children must be "free to follow their private convictions at an age when they can exercise mature discretion." Coleridge listened with interest and then invited the gentleman to see his garden. Instead of a garden, they discovered a brick wall surrounding an unruly patch of weeds.

"Why, this is not a garden!" the man remarked. "There is nothing here but weeds."

"Well, now," said Coleridge, "I did not want to infringe upon the liberty of the garden in any way. I was just giving the garden a chance to express itself and to choose its own production."

Parents will do well to meditate on the famous instruction from Deuteronomy 6. Moses counseled his people to remember the words that had been given in the law:

> And these words which I command you this day shall be upon your heart; and you shall teach them diligently to your children, and shall talk of them when you sit in your house, and when you walk by the way, and when you lie down, and when you rise. And you shall bind them as a sign upon your hand, and they shall be as frontlets between your eyes. And you shall write them on the doorposts of your house and on your gates. (Deut 6:6-9)

There is a profound wisdom in the practice that is outlined here. It suggests a number of ways that we make the Bible a daily part of our family's life. Wherever we turn, whatever we do, there are several creative ways to confront ourselves and our children with the Word of God.

Martin Luther, as avid and disciplined as he was in study, would sometimes work with children playing around his feet. If they became too loud, he said, he would warn them sternly and then they would return to a more moderate level of singing and playing. But occasionally, he said, he would stop, take Hans up on his lap and "teach him a lesson." By that he meant, of course, he would teach him something from Scripture.

Children do not have an inborn bias against learning from

the Bible.They are avid learners; they are curious about all sorts
of things. And the Bible is a literal treasury of fascinating subjects. The parents, without being falsely pious and too precious
about the whole thing, can teach children the Bible as easily
and naturally as they teach them to tie their shoes, eat with a
fork and spell "C-A-T."

In addition, however, several more regular practices can help
to keep us consistent in what we try to do. I am going to suggest
some of these practices that might be used with children in
broad age ranges. Use these practices in the way that seems
most suitable, practical and natural for your own family. Adapt
them to your own circumstances. Add to them any method or
approach that seems to accomplish the same purpose. Above
all, do not treat them as deadly serious, legal observances. The
secret is to teach children to enjoy the Bible; and when they
see that you enjoy an approach to Scripture, the fun becomes
contagious.

Infants and Preschoolers

The mother of a five-year-old asked her pastor when she
should start religious training with her child. The minister
asked how old the child was and then said, "You are already
five years late in getting started."

The time to begin Christian training for children is the very
first year of their lives. Children learn about the love of God
from the love of their parents. When they later hear of God
referred to as a heavenly Father, the content they give to that
name will largely depend on their experience with an earthly
father. From their earliest days children take the actions, words
and tone of voice of their parents (and a few others) as clues
to the nature of their world.

Abraham Heschel's *Man Is Not Alone* contains a chapter entitled "The World Is an Allusion." All of the world, he shows,
points to a glory that suffuses and yet transcends it. The home,
filled with love, becomes a way of alluding to those truths that
a child learns more explicitly in the Bible. At the same time,
even those earliest days, weeks and months can have a telling

effect on the way a child at an older age comprehends the message of God's love.

Most important in these early years is developing and directing the imagination. We all live by our imaginations, even though adults may lose touch with that fact. Imagination is not just the way we perceive unreal things; it is the way we perceive everything. The way we direct our conscious mind, the way we mentally organize our world, the way we respond to things depends on those mental *images* that are developed from the time of our birth. So the earliest exercises related to the Bible should help the child develop a God-centered and Bible-enriched imagination.

Richard Foster, in *Celebration of Discipline,* says, "Imagination opens the door to faith." Our ability to integrate the world, mentally and emotionally, in such a way that it becomes apparent that God has a hand in the matter of this world, depends on the power and richness of imagination. George Bernard Shaw's Joan of Arc was told that the voice of God she heard was only her imagination. "Yes," she said, "that is how God speaks to me."

A skeptic can, of course, say that such intentions are only training a child to believe in things that are normally unbelievable, to perceive that which is unreal. I am immediately reminded of C. S. Lewis's comment that a savage can see a copy of one of the greatest poems in the English language and only see it as black marks on a page. His unaided imagination will see no more. Is the person that is trained to read (through the use of a highly cultivated imagination) and then to appreciate good poetry (through an even more highly cultivated imagination) thus trained to perceive something that really is not there? Certainly not. A Wordsworth, an Auden and an Eliot do not produce less *real* poetry because it takes a trained sensitivity and imaginative taste to discern it. Rather the truth is the other way around: a highly cultivated imagination helps us to perceive what left to unaided nature we would miss entirely.

How, then, can we help even small children develop imaginations enriched by the Bible? How can we help them begin to see, as the biblical writers themselves saw, that "the heavens are telling the glory of God; and the firmament proclaims his handiwork" (Ps 19:1).

At the earliest age a way of cultivating the imagination is simply to show pictures from an illustrated children's Bible. Let the child hear the names "David," "Daniel" and "Jesus." Place names like Bethlehem, Jerusalem, Shiloh and Gilgal should become familiar sounds.

Children sometimes love to pore over pictures and take in the details. The parent who waits patiently while the child enjoys a feast of the soul will sometimes find that he has learned to imagine his way into the biblical story.

The Bible story naturally overlaps one of the most important aspects of early learning. Just as Adam was called on to name the animals and objects in his world, infants strive to give out a sound that represents the creatures that they see both in art and in life. The simple message that "All things bright and beautiful,/All creatures great and small,/All things wise and wonderful,/The Lord God made them all" is the first and last lesson that we ever learn. And it is one that an inventive mother or father can teach in a thousand different ways.

Many parents read Bible stories from children's versions of the Bible from the first year of a child's life. May their numbers increase. However, I would like to suggest an even better way of doing the same thing. That is, *tell the story,* rather than read it. This approach requires, of course, that you read the story first and absorb as many details and as many dramatic elements as possible. If you make this special effort at preparation (which really doesn't take much time, after all), then you will be surprised at the ease with which you can make the story come to life.

Many parents can put more dramatic appeal into a story that is told than into one that is read. And you might be surprised at how attentive children can be to a story that comes directly from the parent instead of from the pages of a book. The point is to put your own imagination to work in order to enrich that of your children. These stories need not (in fact, should not)

be a rigid recital of facts. Don't hesitate to describe how hard
Goliath fell when David stunned him with one of his little
smooth stones, or how frightened the little lamb was whose
shepherd searched for him in the wilderness. Tell the Bible
stories from different points of view. For instance, in recounting the story of the shepherd and the lost sheep, tell the story
from the lamb's point of view. Or tell the story of Isaac's birth
from Sarah's perspective.

Parables have a natural appeal to small children. Many of
them are simple stories with obvious opportunities to play on
the dramatic and tragic elements in life. Parents can include
these in their repertoire of nighttime stories. When she was
three years old, my daughter's favorite stories—the ones she
wanted to hear repeatedly—involved the prodigal son, the lost
sheep, and the importunate neighbor.

In addition, the Old Testament presents us with a whole
library of tales to choose from. Children often find that their
favorite stories are those about Moses delivering the people of
Israel from Pharaoh's bondage, or David confronting Goliath,
Jonah's attempt to escape his mission, Elijah's challenge to the
priests of Baal, and Daniel's night in a den of lions. It should
be no surprise that these stories have the ability to hold and
inspire a young child. Long before written materials were plen-
tiful these were the tales told around a family hearth to the rapt
attention of old and young alike. They have the tone and structure of tales passed from generation to generation by word of
mouth. Even long after they were written down, the most common way of spreading these stories was by an oral recounting.
It is no wonder that many of your most successful attempts to
get the Bible across will be through casual retelling of the stories to young children who will hear them and then request
them again and again.

One warning. There are many things that can be done in the
telling and retelling of Bible stories. They can be straight or
imaginative. They can be told from a variety of points of view—
even Jonah's story from the whale's point of view! But one
thing turns the story into something it was never intended to

be—and that one thing parents are often tempted to do—and that is to tag the story with a "moral." The very reason for the story is that it tells more than a moral statement ever could. It is many-faceted; it has an atmosphere and a variety of implications. To boil it down to a simple moral robs a story of the very attraction and power it has for children. It makes no difference that poor Sunday-school curriculum tries to do this very thing. The story of the prodigal son gives one a feeling of the benevolent and forgiving father; it demonstrates the wisdom of confession; and it anticipates the moral relief of forgiveness. To add to that magnificent story a comment such as "So the moral is: Our heavenly Father always receives us gladly no matter how far we have strayed," renders the whole affair so flat and powerless that what began as drama and a tale of the enormous attractiveness of redemption ends as trivia.

Why did Jesus speak to the crowds only in parables? Perhaps because he wanted them to understand the most that they could understand. And though his disciples benefited from explanation, those who had never reached a mature stage had to learn first what the gospel feels like in the subtle allusion of parables. Children, too, need to have their world filled out and populated with figures and events in which the gospel can take root. Stories—all by themselves, if they are the right stories—can accomplish that purpose without the weak support of "the moral of this story is . . ."

Schoolchildren

Older children benefit from some of the same things that younger ones do. But with older children there are more things you can do. When a child is five or six is a good time to engage in family games that center around Bible knowledge. Some of these can be purchased from any good Christian bookstore, but made-up games are often just as effective. A great amount of interest can be generated by having a simple Bible quiz around the dinner table. See how many questions can be answered correctly out of ten or twenty. Play "twenty questions" by having a Bible character or city in mind and allowing the children twenty questions in order to discover the name or place that you have in mind.

Encourage children to memorize passages from the Bible. Start with small passages like John 3:16. Soon they will easily be learning Psalms 1, 19 and 23, or 1 Corinthians 13. You may use rewards of different types if this seems to work well with your children, but many children find the achievement of mastering a beautiful passage of Scripture a reward that far exceeds a gift of money or a gold star by their names. However, do recognize and rejoice with them in their victory over the task of memorizing Scripture.

Adolescents

Teen-agers are beginning to take on the responsibility of adulthood. Their involvement in Bible study may not be significantly different from that of adults. Their study is more likely to be self-motivated and self-guided. But there are a few matters that parents should keep in mind as they encourage and guide their teen-agers in Bible study.

1. *Adolescence is a time in which inherited beliefs are put to the test.* Rarely are the beliefs of normally loving Christian parents radically rejected by their children in adulthood. But try telling this to a parent who sees his teen-ager dabbling in everything from Zen Buddhism to standard atheism within two weeks' time. Anyone who has tried to console a Christian parent whose teen-ager now refuses to attend church or whose child attends only under protest, sitting through the worship in a great pout, knows how difficult it is to convince these parents that perhaps it isn't all their fault—and perhaps this isn't the final stage of the teen-ager's personality development.

The secret to helping teen-agers develop their knowledge and understanding of the Bible parallels the parents' role in other areas. The close and specific direction needed by a younger child is not needed by the teen-ager. To a reasonable extent the best approach is to stand aside and watch it happen. Because, after all, even the doubt and disorganizing of all the former certainties in life is a part of an overall constructive

process. These young men and women are arriving—awkward-
ly, gravely, dangerously—at their own beliefs. The time when
honest life can be sustained on borrowed beliefs is past. They
must find the solid rock that lies beneath all the accumulation
of childhood training and Sunday-school lessons.

The building blocks of childhood will be examined one by
one to see if they will serve their purposes as they build new
adult lives. Some blocks will be discarded too quickly. Some will
be maintained that should have been set aside, along with the
doll clothes and train sets. But only by this peril-filled process—
while parents look on anxiously—can adolescents build a life
that will stand the tests that adult life will inevitably bring.

2. *The parents' role in Bible study is that of an example and an
adviser.* Example should be stressed because—while teen-agers
are busily building their new adult lives—they have an overwhelming interest in observing patterns that they find in adult
life. The pattern of adult life set by parents is the one closest
at hand, and though teen-agers may be loath to admit it, they
will likely use the patterns of their mothers and fathers more
than any other. Parents who cultivate their own interest in the
Bible will often—without even trying—cultivate the interests of
their young son or daughter.

Adviser can also be stressed if we understand that to be the
kind of adviser any normal adult would seek out—namely, one
who advises us when we intentionally ask for it and not one
who forces the issue in an unwelcome manner.

Of course, teen-agers are still, in large part, children. And
they need more direction than adults should usually need.
Ideally, parents will want to allow their teen-agers to build their
own lives. But at the same time they should be standing by,
ready to hand them a good brick when they call for it. Their
role is not to shout from the sidelines or to take over the job.
Most of all, the parents' role is not to suppress the honest
expression of doubt or experimentation in ideas and beliefs. As
destructive as the whole process may appear to be, we can
surely believe that adolescence, with all of its normally bizarre
psychological, intellectual and emotional manifestations, is a

God-ordained experience. And although childhood assurances may crumble, the edifice that is built in its place will not likely be all that different from what seemed to be building as childhood progressed. But it will be larger, and it will be one in which an adult can live.

Most of these occasions to advise teen-agers and guide them in Bible study will be met with the fruits of parents' own study. But there are some standard parts of the Scripture that should come to mind when the teen-ager brings up specific matters that are typical concerns.

For instance, the problem of pain and suffering in a world created by a loving God is one of the most serious questions that believers face at every age. Parents should be ready to direct the young person to the book of Job, that greatest of all treatments of the problem of suffering.

How should we think about human destiny in general? Of that of Christians? What difference does it make in our daily lives? No better passage could come to mind than Jesus' teachings in Matthew 24 and 25.

This teaching is often related in our minds to the question of our personal, private destiny. What happens to those who die as Christians? Direct them to 1 Corinthians 15.

Young adults or adolescents who are in earnest in their commitment to Jesus Christ want to know how to discern God's will for their lives. A thoughtful reading of 1 John 4 will lead to a number of insights into finding and recognizing God's will in every area of life.

For basic moral conduct, teen-agers should find their way through the Proverbs. With regard to the forgiveness of others, they need to be acquainted with Matthew 18:21-35. Forgiveness from God finds no higher statement than that of Luke 15. The nature and reality of sin are treated aspect by aspect in Genesis 3—11 and Romans 1—3. How can teen-agers find encouragement in the fierce battle against temptation? Two passages that might come to mind are 1 Corinthians 10:13 and Romans 8:35-39.

Teen-agers should not be encouraged to see these passages

as "answers" to their questions. Job, after all, does not come across with a packaged answer to the problem of pain and human suffering. Rather—like all of the highest expressions of biblical thought—this account brings us into a relationship, it sets things into their proper context, so that we can begin to think about the problem in a mature and productive way. The answer, after all, is not something apart from God, it is God himself. Paul pleaded for relief from the "thorn in the flesh"; what he received was grace. In other words, he prayed for an answer, and he got more than an answer. He received more of God himself, which is greater than any answer could have been.

Adolescents should begin to make this kind of distinction in their own thinking. One of the greatest barriers and discouragements that we could put in the way of their real understanding of Scripture is to make it less than it really is. To make it an answer book, where we put in our quarter's worth of questions, pull the knob and get out a neatly packaged answer, is selling the Book short. Teen-agers are looking for adult answers. And the greatest thing about this Bible, the thing that will turn them on to it for the rest of their lives, is that it is a book that will cause them to stretch their vision and help them grow up to an adult-sized view of life. This begins to happen when they see that it does not simply lead them to answers but to the Answer; that the particular truths in the Bible lead to a personal and ultimate truth; that the words of the Bible lead to that inexpressible and personal Word of God.

The Power of the Word and the Life of the Family
Richard Weaver said: "All . . . community depends upon the ability of men to understand one another."[1]

This principle is no less true, perhaps even more true, of the family than any other kind of community.

But it is precisely this matter of community that is so difficult to communicate. It is made up of invisible things, like unconditional love, trust, sympathy. Even these words are abstractions for something we feel. Just to name the feeling is hardly to describe it. The sensuous, of course, is more easily described, and it catches our attention quickly: thus, much public expression dwells on that aspect of personality. The higher qualities and the rarer ones are not so easily defined, but they are the ones a family lives by.

That is why the Bible is, as much here as anywhere, indispensable. Only a book thus inspired—breathed on by the creator of the family himself—could put such sinews and such firm features on the very qualities that make life in a family the closest earthly imitation of life in the kingdom of heaven.

Has it become clear then that I believe that the Bible is important to the family for a reason that is vastly greater than the fact that it contains good instruction for the family? That it certainly has—and in abundance. But beyond that very practical and important consideration is a matter of greater importance. By way of the Bible, the family meets life on a common field of thought and sentiment. And, moreover, that common experience with which they meet the world around them is none other than an experience of the God who created them a family. The very God who sealed the marriage, the very God who blessed it with children, addresses them in the pages of the Bible. Here, as nowhere else, those qualities so essential to the family become real and compelling. Here, as nowhere else, people come into contact with the creative love that causes them to belong uniquely to one another.

11
Bible Study in the Church

As is true of the family, though on a different level, the church is responsible for making the Word of God the language of the people of God.

Who could doubt, however, that the job has often been riddled with inadequacies and failures? Can it be shown, for instance, in most churches today, that over a period of time the congregation has generally gained a greater knowledge of Scripture?

Students are constantly telling me that in a survey course of the New Testament—the first and most elementary introduction to New Testament studies—they run across a great many things about the New Testament that they had never encountered in fifteen to twenty years in the church. One hopes, of course, that they learn something new in an undergraduate course, but I have a feeling that the gap in biblical literacy is much wider than it ought to be.

Teachers of English tell me that their students have difficulty with writers like John Milton, Nathaniel Hawthorne and Herman Melville because they don't understand the many biblical allusions. In a chapter on "The Tail" for instance, Melville's

Moby Dick tells of how the whale always turns his tail on man
rather than facing him directly. Subtly Melville makes the whale
analogous to God and says (without quotation marks), "Thou
shalt see my back parts, my tail, he seems to say, but my face
shall not be seen."[1] To an earlier age, more biblically literate,
this is a clear reference to Moses' experience in Exodus 33 and
the very words of verse 23 in that chapter. But to our generation, far too often, the allusion is missed altogether.

But the most disturbing part of this is that my friends on the
English faculty tell me that there is hardly any difference, in
this respect, between those students who have attended church
most of their lives and those who have not. Pause now and ask,
What have we done with those wasted years? What indeed, even
if we have taught them the same salvation formula or the same
moral lessons twenty-five times a year for years on end? And
then we wonder why their training does not sustain them
through early adulthood, when we've never really taught them
what substance and solid experience stands *behind* those moral
and missionary conclusions. They simply haven't learned the
Bible itself.

What I want to put forward in this chapter is a series of
suggestions aimed at making the Bible known within the
church. The suggestions are not novel, but several of them are
essential to bringing about any kind of effective reconstruction
in biblical teaching.

Pastoral Priorities and Bible Study

"Our pastor does his homework" is a glowing compliment from
parishioners who know that if their pastor is *not* doing his
homework then *their* time in the pew on Sunday morning is at
least partly wasted. Here is one reason I deeply appreciate my
own pastor—he does his homework, and it is evident that he
does. His teaching is substantial, and it bears the conviction of
one who has spent time wrestling with scriptural content.

But I also know that he often does that in the very teeth of
modern evangelical church expectations that frequently crowd
out any good quality time for study. Seldom would anyone say

that the pastor's study time is not important, and most church members really estimate the value of their church experience on the basis of what happens Sunday morning, Sunday evening and Wednesday. Yet they and their pastor give priority to so many other things that the inevitable result is to steal time from the less public responsibility of study.

Most parishioners don't really care to spend their Sundays listening to warmed-over banalities from a minister who simply had too many other demands during the week to allow adequate study for his sermon. I would venture to say that it would make good sense to most church members to expect that the pastor would be first and foremost a student of Scripture and that he would also be well acquainted with related disciplines—theology, Christian philosophy, history, ethics, literature. His job is to know and proclaim and teach and defend the gospel message in the most effective manner possible.

Regardless of the habits that churches have grown into, I think most parishioners would not consider it heresy if the pastor were absolved of a major part of administrative responsibilities. Thousands of well-run organizations in this country operate on the local level with no professional administrative staff. Is it not also possible that churches could well do the same without the often quasi-professional administrative leadership of the pastor?

In Southern Baptist churches we often have long interim periods between outgoing and incoming pastors. In these cases laymen or other staff members take over the administrative duties that the pastor had shouldered himself; and I have never noticed that a church was administratively disadvantaged by the change. Sometimes it was a decided improvement! Yet as soon as the new minister is installed, the housekeeping duties are shifted back to his office thus signaling to everyone how we expect the pastor to spend his time.

If a building program is in progress, for instance, the pastor should be so uninvolved that he doesn't know it's over until they ask him to preach in a new sanctuary. The planning, promotion, coordinating can be altogether done by other (and more professionally competent) members of the congregation. Some churches are large enough to have staff members who are talented and trained in administration, and the freedom this leaves the pastor for his spiritual and biblical ministry shows how wise this division of labor can be. But the same type of thing can be done on a smaller scale, in smaller churches, by employing the native and trained talents of lay people.

Pastoral Priorities and Theological Education

If we are serious about reconstructing the church as an effective community for Bible learning, then we really need to start even further back in the process. Fortunately, seminaries can provide a good opportunity to learn important skills in ministry. Homiletics, pastoral counseling, the educational programs of the church, church administration, and a dozen other matters require some introduction and even training to the point of competency.

But when these professional skill courses begin to displace a substantial curriculum in Old Testament, New Testament, theology, languages and history, then there might be reason to question whether ministers are really being adequately prepared to deal with the life-and-death issues which are the real focus of their calling. Lay people, after all, look to pastors for guidance in answering some of the most basic questions of life. If they cannot deal with these questions with some evidence of depth, and if they cannot appeal to biblical authority as one who knows the Bible, then all of their program ideas and counseling skills and administrative competency cannot serve to justify their right to stand behind the pulpit and proclaim the Word that means life to their congregations.

The answer to this need is obvious: a reversal of the trend toward an expanded curriculum in professional skills and a renewed stress on courses that promote biblical and theological competency. The danger signs and the need for this reversal are already evident when one can find dozens of seminary graduates in any city—and I have met several—whose seminary training was lacking in any course that focused on one book of the Bible (as opposed to a survey of several books) and who have never read the works of even one major theologian. No wonder too many college students I know feel they cannot find substantial answers to their questions in the church.

Bible Study and the Intellectual Climate of the Church

From the very beginning the church has appealed to the common people. Even, and sometimes especially, it has reached out to the "unwashed and unlearned." In an important sense, the church can only be true to its own character by giving a central place to concern for the poor, the outcast and those deserted by other elements of society. If we do not believe *all* human beings have infinite worth, then we do not have good news for *any* person, rich or poor.

So we have rightly made the gospel intelligible to those with even the least interest or aptitude for intellectual pursuits. May we continue to do so.

However, this important emphasis can also be used as a disguise for intellectual laziness and anti-intellectual bigotry. Mark's Gospel says of Jesus' teaching that "the great throng heard him gladly" (Mk 12:37). But Mark's observation comes just after Jesus had made a quite subtle point about the Messiah's relationship to David in answer to the scribes—the Jewish bookmen or scholars of the day. Even the unlearned are gratified to know that the matters of their faith can stand the test of the intellectual arena.

It is fairly obvious, of course, that the study of the Bible is an intellectual endeavor. That is not all it is; it also involves the affections and the heart's receptivity to the things of God; it involves a spiritual alertness and a moral commitment. But it *does* involve the mental ordering of facts and events, critical skills of a high order, and the willingness to engage in sustained mental effort.

These matters cannot simply be put down as being of interest only to an intellectual elite whose activities have no bearing on the practical, everyday affairs of the church. Take, for instance, the problem presented to the Christian theist on the existence of evil: If God is altogether good he does not want evil; and if he is altogether powerful, he could make a world without evil. So the question is—why is there evil? Is God *not* good? Or is he *not* all powerful? Some of the best minds in Christian civilization have wrestled with that question. But it is hardly an exercise exclusively for the intelligentsia. I have heard the question of the problem of evil posed by a woman with no formal education in the foothills of eastern Kentucky. And I have heard the question from children. And these people are not indifferent to someone dealing with this question seriously and competently.

The high-water mark of intellectual endeavor in the church also has a bearing on the lives of those who drink from the distant tributaries, and the church has almost always recognized that fact. In the early centuries of the church two remarkable trends became evident. One was the ability of the gospel to win the hearts and loyalties of the poor, to lift the dispossessed out of their gray existence and render their lives transfused in the light of the gospel. The other trend was the wholesale conversion of philosophers, thinkers and great university centers like Alexandria to Christianity. Early leaders of the church, such as Tertullian, Origen and Augustine were great lovers of God, compassionate servants and moving preachers, but they were also great thinkers, known for their learning and their skill in the learned disciplines.

If the church is to recover its ability to teach the Bible, even to those who have no interest and little aptitude for scholarship, it must prove itself capable of contending for the faith in the marketplace of contemporary thought. There is, of course, a great abundance of that sort of proof in the world today. One can hardly miss the fact that, among the most vigorous and impressive intellects today are Christians of the stature of Paul Ricoeur, Jacques Ellul, Aleksandr Solzhenitsyn, Malcolm Muggeridge and a considerable number of others. But on the level of denominational and congregational work there is too often a great timidity about dealing with intellectual issues.

I think this comes less from an inability to do so than from a certain sense that to appeal to the intelligentsia is to abandon the concerns of the common people. We are hampered more by democratic sentiment than by the demands of the gospel, however. And what too often results from this timidity in the arena of ideas is that the great, broad, middle group of intelligent, thoughtful people—many of them young adults of college age or a little older—are allowed to think that the simplistic answers they hear in church and read in church literature are really representative of the highest expression of Christian thought. They are not, of course; and they never have been. But because the churches fear to leave out those not motivated to intellectual pursuits, they abandon the difficult questions posed by those who would really like to know if the Christian faith can give a credible account of its view.

James Orr pointed out that this was hardly the traditional posture of the church in matters regarding learning:

It has been frequently remarked that in pagan religions the doctrinal element is at a minimum—the chief thing there is the performance of a ritual. But this is precisely where Christianity distinguishes itself from other religions—it does contain doctrine. It comes to men with definite, positive teaching; it claims to be the truth; it bases religion on knowledge which is only attainable under moral conditions. . . . A religion divorced from earnest and lofty thought has always, down the whole history of the church, tended to become weak, jejune and unwholesome; while the intellect, deprived of its rights within religion, has sought its satisfaction without, and developed into godless rationalism.[2]

Our faith has always grown outward from that central commitment of the Old Testament religion "to love God with all one's soul"—which includes, of course, loving God with one's intellectual faculties. Without a continued commitment to discipleship in that area, the first casualty of the church will be Bible study in any true sense—but along with that will fall evangelism, missions and every active concern of the church.

What is required here is that church leaders refrain from underestimating the intellectual tastes and the seriousness of the questions of Christian people. And, second, they must become willing to risk the free exchange of thought on important questions that face the world and challenge Christian philosophy and theology; only then do people have the opportunity of seeing that Christian thought is capable of meeting the general world of thought on better than equal terms.

Coordinating Efforts for Effective Bible Study

If our task is to make the gospel known and if the gospel is the message of the Bible, I wonder, when I stop to look at what we actually do, whether we really take our aim seriously. The sermon texts from week to week are often likely to be random selections of interest to the pastor. So the congregation is fed a slice of Job, followed by a word study from 1 Corinthians, and then a dose of Romans. Worse yet is the sermon that hardly relates to the text at all; it seems as if the text were selected as a suitable ornament to grace the minister's lofty thoughts.

Central biblical doctrines are missed altogether in this process, especially the doctrines of sin and repentance, although we can look back to a time bereft of clear teachings on grace and forgiveness. And I'm not even sure that today—though grace and forgiveness enjoy some popularity—that they are understood in a biblical frame of reference.

The Sunday-school classes and other organizations are, meantime, going on their own way with little thought of the doctrinal preoccupations of the pulpit. So in addition to Job and Romans, church attenders might also get a smattering of James or Titus. Their minds are offered a great smorgasbord of facts, notions, Christian attitudes, moral platitudes, as well as sound—but slightly undigested—teaching. These disparate impressions don't stick very long, because there has been no effort to present biblical teaching in a manner that is clear, progressive and well organized.

No one would ever expect to learn a foreign language or history or mathematics in such a way, but when it comes to teaching the language of faith we are often left to the mercy of pure chance and desultory efforts.

The local church congregation is the natural place to begin reconstructing our approach to teaching the Bible. The pulpit preaching should lead the whole process through a clear and orderly presentation of biblical teaching. This should often take the form of preaching through, over a period of time, a single book of the Bible. Some pastors do this and maintain a balance by preaching from the New Testament in the morning worship service and preaching from a book of the Old Testament on Sunday night or on other occasions.

But preaching through a book is not the only way this clear, ordered presentation can take place. Sometimes a smaller, but significant, text can be the focus of a series of preaching events. The Sermon on the Mount or the Ten Commandments would be likely texts for this kind of close focus. On occasions the minister may want to trace the biblical teachings on a particular doctrine. Then he would follow, in some systematic order, the biblical themes on Christology, or the doctrine of the Spirit, or the doctrine of man.

From this central point of a clearly defined progression of pulpit emphases, other teaching opportunities can be used to increase and reinforce the exposure to biblical content.

Where the church Bible study program is tied to a certain line of curriculum, the pastor could coordinate his preaching to match the progression of teaching in these lessons.

Otherwise, small Bible study groups meeting at times other than Sunday morning can be employed to carry further the teaching emphasis that is set by the preaching. Several small groups, organized around common interests, can then make a more concerted effort to get at the heart of the Scripture that was the text for Sunday's sermon.

Additionally, the pastor can suggest and even publish a list of readings that would be helpful to the congregation in doing their own independent, or small group, study of the text.

The point is that a coordinated effort at Bible study leads to a number of advantages in actually teaching the Bible to church people. The first most obvious matter is that everyone is exposed, hopefully more than once, to the Scripture under consideration. Sharing this common emphasis throughout the church in several settings over a period of time, and with opportunities to share our thoughts with others, heightens the general awareness of the teachings involved.

There is no comparison between the two experiences. On the one hand is that of a church spending a full month in the book of James, with small study groups handling most of the individual questions, with encouragement on every hand to actually *read* the entire book of James, and with the whole process coordinated and led by a pulpit ministry that takes seriously the need to teach the Bible. On the other hand is the more typical experience of hearing a text read from James and commented upon, perhaps once during the year.

If the local church intends to teach the Bible, then every teaching opportunity it is given should reflect the fact that it is in earnest.

Sincerity and Bible Study

Mark Rutherford wrote of someone, "He was as sincere as he could be, and yet no religious expression of his was ever so sincere as the most ordinary expression of the most trifling pleasure or pain."[3]

I could not conclude this section without making some reference to what seems to be most needed. If the church has been ineffective in promoting Bible literacy among people, its most significant deficiency has not been in its method or its program, but in a certain lack of sincerity.

I do not mean that church leaders have acted as charlatans or that they have deliberately attempted to deceive. I don't believe that any more than I believe Jesus accused the Pharisees of that kind of hypocrisy: they were hypocrites even though they may have earnestly wanted to be otherwise. So modern churches—and I have in mind evangelical churches in particular—believe earnestly in the Bible, and they want to promote its teachings, and they want to convince others of the authority of the Bible. But somehow the words lack conviction because the experience of the Bible as a guiding intellectual force and a formative spiritual influence simply has not been there.

What we have plenty of is sentimentalism concerning the Bible. But this is hardly the same as moral conviction that is born of struggling with basic questions, taking on oneself the yoke of disciplined study, and waiting with humility until light breaks upon the interpretation of a difficult passage.

D. H. Lawrence implied that sentimentalism is more self-deception than anything else:

> Sentimentalism is the working off on yourself of feelings you haven't really got. We all *want* to have certain feelings: feelings of love, of passionate sex, of kindliness and so forth. Very few people really feel love, or sex passion, or kindliness, or anything else that goes at all deep. So the mass just fake these feelings inside themselves. Faked feelings! The world is all gummy with them.[4]

The tacit obligation to express feelings in church that we really haven't got is sentimentalism. More than one observer of American churches has commented on how we habitually express excitement in a manner that makes one believe "he doth protest too much."

But this distinction becomes critical when we apply it to Bible study. Sentimentalism jumps to conclusions and imposes them on the text; sincerity suffers more for the truth and reserves judgment on matters of uncertainty. Sentimentalism demands that we have all the answers instantly and will not admit to doubt; sincerity is thankful for the little it does know and is patient with doubt—thus expressing faith. Sentimentalism convinces Christians of the sins of others; sincerity convicts them of their own. Sentimentalism loves most to interpret the Bible and apply it to life; sincerity wants to experience life and finds the Bible a reliable guide to interpret that experience. Sentimentalism loves the idea of loving the Bible; sincerity loves the Bible as a true gift from God.

In short, sincerity is that intellectual, moral and spiritual directness that comes when one has paid a price for the truth. The church can never convince the world of Bible truth until it has become convinced through the real discipline of study.

12
Bible Study
and
World Missions

Then they said, "*Come, let us build ourselves a city, and a tower with its top in the heavens, and let us make a name for ourselves, lest we be scattered abroad upon the face of the whole earth.*" *And the LORD came down to see the city and the tower, which the sons of men had built. And the LORD said,* "*Behold, they are one people, and they have all one language; and this is only the beginning of what they will do; and nothing that they propose to do will now be impossible for them. Come, let us go down, and there confuse their language, that they may not understand one another's speech.*" *(Gen 11:4-7)*

Now there were dwelling in Jerusalem Jews, devout men from every nation under heaven. And at this sound the multitude came together, and they were bewildered, because each one heard them speaking in his own language. (Acts 2:5-6)

My first title for this book was *A Grammar of Faith,* and it was subtitled *The Theory and Practice of Bible Study.* The notion for this title came to me from John Henry Newman's *A Grammar of Assent,* a book on the meaning of religious belief. It struck me that this fortunate phrase easily suggests the role the Bible plays in various dimensions of life.

In much the same way grammar serves language, the Bible

serves faith. Grammar does not create language, but it reveals its structure and force. The Bible does not create faith, only the Spirit of God can do that, but it does bring faith within reach and present it in such a way that the Spirit can make that faith ours. Grammar gives us a grasp of language and shows its inner workings, though it cannot dispel all the mystery of language. The Bible displays the great moments of faith so that it sets the standard for viewing life through the eyes of faith. A formal grammar allows language to find its center and to recognize the irregular, even to diagnose the deviant and subversive phrase. The Bible works in a similar way for religion.

Above all, however, a formal grammar allows language to be understood *in the same way* by a large number of people. It assures that it is a common language—that it does, in fact, communicate.

When we were visiting in London, my wife read in the *Times* that a linguist had predicted that by the year 2025 the English and Americans will no longer be able to understand each other. Their uses of language, he said, are more and more distinct and are following separate courses. They will eventually drift so far apart that they will be speaking virtually two quite different languages.

If that does not happen (and somehow I don't really expect it), then it will be because they both adhere to the same standards of grammar. Grammar, as it is formally presented in books of grammar and as it is understood through grammatical rules, is something that unifies people and keeps them speaking the same language.

When I think of the Bible as a grammar of faith, I am thinking particularly of its role in missions. The Bible plays a more positive role than the grammatical rules of a language. It allows us to reach out to people who are already of diverse languages, if by "language" we can include not only our ways of speaking but our ways of expressing the experience of life. By telling people what *has* happened, the Bible also tells them what *is* happening to them and to the world they live in. By telling of a common beginning, it provides a basis for mutual compassion. By speaking of a universal destiny, it holds out the possibility of a common hope.

The Confusion of Tongues

It is most appropriate today to think of the Bible in this way. We live in a world of confused tongues. That is what the Genesis story of the tower of Babel is all about. And the curse of Babel has never been more apparent than it is today. Because of sin, people are divided. And they are divided by language. But more than that, and at a level for which language is only an outward sign, they are divided in their ways of thinking, feeling and seeing.

> Oh, East is East, and West is West,
>   and never the twain shall meet,
> Till Earth and Sky stand presently
>   at God's great Judgment Seat.[1]

In addition to language, race and culture, all of which mark off boundaries among us, there are the divisions created by ideologies and moral persuasions.

Nothing should surprise us more than that these divisions are increasingly evident at a time when modern technology has made it possible to communicate on a wider scale more conveniently than ever before. We are more likely to know people from nations halfway around the world, to have traveled that far ourselves, and to know a greater number from different nations than was likely even three or four decades ago. While we become inured to the strangeness of other cultures, we are constantly baffled by some new ideology, or a religious cult somewhere in Oregon that sprang up like dandelions. The more our world shrinks and the more we talk, the more it becomes evident that we don't speak the same language even if everyone agrees to speak English!

Within one nation the plurality of moral standards has perhaps never been more evident than today. We speak of it constantly. Colleges offer courses on values clarification. Television talk shows highlight discussions of moral choices. Yet once more it becomes evident that our talk gets us nowhere. We do not begin with the same principles or with the same way of seeing the world, and our much desired openness leads only to isolation and estrangement.

What we see happening in the West, that had once found a measure of unity in its common faith, is the re-emergence of paganism. The pagan world was ruled by many gods. Nations did not share common origins or common destinies; they did not belong to the same world. In a sense our new paganism is worse. Not only are we divided according to nations, within which are found a homogenous culture, but people are divided into even smaller groups, isolated by ideologies and partisan spirit.

Materialistic values, so prevalent in the West, heighten the crisis, because here it becomes increasingly possible for the individuals to focus only on themselves. Narcissism, greed and sensuality end in the isolation of the individual from all forms of society including the family. This results in a larger number of people than ever before who live without any significant social ties. The film of modern Western life casts its image across the screen, an image of actors bravely convincing themselves that a life free from social obligation, given over to sensual and narcissistic freedom, is the "real thing" and that it is "filled with gusto." But when the lights die down, the chatter ceases, the frenetic music stops, and each individual withdraws within himself, a pall of despair fills the atmosphere. There is no solitude—which might speak richly of the presence of God—only a desperate loneliness. All live in their own world, with their own gods and make a pathetic attempt to live their lives according to the superstitious canons of self-sufficiency.

The pagan world was distinct from the Christian world because it had not yet caught the vision of the world's one destiny and one origin in the one and only God. The world as it stands apart from the Word of God is always a world fractured, divided and alienated. Such was the lesson of the Babel story in Genesis. That story, brief though it is, stands as a summary comment on a world in which God's redemptive Word had not yet found an Abraham. It had not yet found its first missionary. But there we begin to see that what this Word did in biblical history is what it intends to do even today.

The Reconciling Word in Biblical History

Without this unifying Word, the people of the world fashioned their own gods, giving expression to the belief that their world was the only world—and the world of all those others with their alien gods and alien tongues did not exist in any real human sense.

Both gods and people could be tolerant of religious divisions. Zeus could live side by side with Baal and Astarte. Nor would they quarrel with the existence of Seth and Hathor; Marduk, Hauron and Rashap were welcome in almost any land's pantheon.

But though they were tolerant, it was not a tolerance that embraced other people as brothers; instead they held each other at arm's length with indifference and often hostility. In a world where many gods existed, there was always the possibility of many worlds and many peoples—and never the necessity of relating these worlds and peoples to each other. Today's West, so enamored of its pluralism, can speak of value systems as if it really did not matter whether society is crisscrossed by altogether different systems that have people living in utterly different worlds.

It was the Hebrews who introduced religious intolerance with their stubborn conviction concerning the existence of one God. All other gods were no gods at all, only evil shadows imitating the power of the *true* God—*their* God. But paradoxically this intolerance toward religious difference made the Hebrews, unlike any other people, grope their way toward the realization that they were specially related to and responsible for all other people on the face of the earth. With one and the same gesture they rejected the gods of the pagans while embracing the pagans themselves.

The Word of God spoken through Israel made it possible for a new conception to dawn on this earth—that the world is one, and people are one, because they belong to the one God.

But there was another important aspect of this development. As long as there were many gods, no one of them could be the author—much less the enforcer—of that moral law which all people acknowledged in one way or another. Religion and morality were two different experiences of life, not always related.

Morality was folk wisdom. Religion was power—especially the power to cope with the elemental forces of nature. The two could be incidentally related, and religion could sometimes be used to enhance the authority of moral law, as in the story of Hammurabi receiving a legal code from the sun-god Shamash. But they were not *necessarily* related. Religion could be unprincipled in the moral realm; and morality could be claimed as the way of human wisdom even when it opposed the ways of the gods. Humankind could be morally right and religiously impotent—that was the making of the tragedy that Greeks discerned so well. Or they could be morally corrupt and religiously potent—those were properly the elements of a farce. But this possibility of the separate realms of morality and religion was the dilemma of paganism. It was left to the Hebrew prophets to fuse into one powerful conviction the two separate experiences of a life morally ordered and one divinely empowered.

In the prophetic vision something really new and crystal clear came along with the concept of monotheism. If there is only one God, then that God is also the author of that rule of life which we all sense and seek to imitate, though we fall short of our ideals. While Zeus and Hera, as well as Baal and Astarte, could only exist under that law, their power and immortality allowed them a certain freedom from it. But this God—one God—is intimately identified with the law. This was a new kind of God, a God of righteousness, who made covenant with his people, demanding righteousness, and promising to write the law upon their hearts (Jer 31:33). No longer the religious cult, but ethical action and righteous attitude became the center of religious concern.

For I desire steadfast love and not sacrifice,
the knowledge of God, rather than burnt
offerings. (Hos 6:6)

He remonstrates against those who "sell the righteous for silver, and the needy for a pair of shoes" or "trample the head of the poor into the dust of the earth, and turn aside the way of the afflicted" (Amos 2:6-7). His cause and the cause of justice—the cause of the rightly ordered life among men—are one and the same. "The Hebrew race," said Matthew Arnold, "found the revelation needed to breathe emotion into the laws of morality, and to make morality religion."[2] This is the God who says, "Cease to do evil, learn to do good; seek justice, correct oppression; defend the fatherless, plead for the widow" (Is 1:16-17). It is to this God that David appeals when he sees that "my sin is ever before me. Against thee, thee only, have I sinned" (Ps 51:3-4).

The Beginning of World Mission

These concepts, as potent and solid as they were at the end of a virtual revolution in thought led by the Hebrew prophets, were concepts almost altogether confined to one nation.

But these developments, as important as they were, proved to be a preparation for the time when the language of monotheism and mono-ethics would become a mighty wind sweeping to the four corners of the earth. The Word of God had become flesh, thus providing the possibility that the presence and power of God would dwell with men and God would pour out his spirit upon all flesh (Joel 2:28).

The story of Babel was reversed at Pentecost. At Babel the rejection of God made unity impossible: apart from God there is no basis for common life, a common vision, a common language. Men and women withdraw into those natural associations of tribes and families, never expand beyond those boundaries and often contract their vision of life to their own solitary souls. Ironically, the one creature who lives for a communion of the spirit with others, dies of solitude and isolation. Their true common language is lost.

At Pentecost, however, it was restored. That is true both literally and, perhaps more important, as a symbol of God's new Word. It is true literally because they each heard the gospel "in his own language" and those from Asia as well as Africa were joined for a moment by the fact that they were addressed by the same words.

It is also true in the sense that the Word of God—the good news that was first preached and then written—was destined to bring people from every quarter, out of every household or nation, into a new fellowship of love and reconciliation.

The Bible and the Mission
That Word spoken to the fractured and alienated world was first an experienced word—experienced by the shores of Galilee, on the road to Damascus, in the Circus Maximus of Rome. It was and is a living language. It communicates and draws people together because it is a common language—a language of deep human need and of insurpassable joy, a language capable of expressing sin and brokenness, but also love and forgiveness. It is a language that moves and changes with the times, that adapts to different cultures and answers to changing circumstances.

The task of Christian missions is to see that language recreated in the hearts and minds of contemporary men and women. The reading of the Bible, the study of the Bible, becomes the key to providing that common language. Missions is more than propagating the gospel message; it is also propagating the gospel in an incarnate fashion. From earliest times it has consisted in giving aid to the poor, providing for the helpless and bringing comfort to the disconsolate. It has meant a service of healing and charity. It has become a visible reality in hospitals, children's homes, schools, rescue missions, homes for unwed mothers, and the list could go on. But the purpose, the raison d'être, for all of these works must be undergirded by a common understanding, a common language.

The missionary enterprise is strongest where the whole church effort focuses on the reading of the Bible. Friends of ours preparing for mission work among Chinese in Malaysia spent their first two years in Taiwan learning the Mandarin dialect of the Chinese language. It was a source of great satisfaction to them that they were learning to speak the one language spoken by more people on earth than any other language. There was open to them now a certain kinship with a part of humanity that was formerly out of reach because of the profound difference in language.

But there was another language that they were bringing to people on the mission field. This language provided the possibility of a common experience, a common view of the world, a story to which all people could relate. That is why the reading of the Bible must remain central to Christian missions, and why it must even be the leading edge. Without that common language, our hospitals, schools and other institutions become so many towers of Babel. They have not the elementary principles, the common focus, and the like affections from which to proceed with a work of good will, even though that work is conceived with the best intentions, and its object is to "reach unto the heavens."

The real basis for world mission is provided in the home and in the local church. The language is spoken among others, the story is told to the nations, but it is learned in the intimate society of those who have made it their language.

I think it is no accident that small Bible study groups have moved into prominence where the gospel is newly taking root. My brother, a fairly new Christian now, has been drawn into the Christian community and finds his principal avenue of growth in an informal Bible study group. College and university students in the United States have, in recent years, become increasingly interested in taking formal classes in New Testament and Old Testament studies. I have taught hundreds of them myself, and I know that seldom do they take the classes for vocational reasons. And many of these are new Christians, or simply students who are wanting to investigate the Bible beliefs.

Any form of Christian mission must recognize that no avenue for propagating the gospel, no expression of the incarnate love of Christ, is unaffected by a lack of Bible knowledge.

"How are men to call upon him in whom they have not

Notes

Chapter One: A Preface to Bible Reading
[1]Mortimer Adler, *How to Read a Book* (New York: Simon & Schuster, 1967), p. 141.
[2]Klaas Runia, *Karl Barth's Doctrine of Holy Scripture* (Grand Rapids, Mich.: Eerdmans, 1962), p. 171.

Chapter Three: The Role of Faith in Bible Reading
[1]Søren Kierkegaard, *Training in Christianity,* trans. by Walter Lowrie (Princeton: Princeton University Press, 1974), p. 140.
[2]Lewis Carroll, *Through the Looking Glass* (New York: Rand McNally & Co., 1916), p. 173.

Chapter Four: A Whole-Bible Strategy
[1]Quoted in George P. Eckman, *The Literary Primacy of the Bible* (New York: The Methodist Book Concern, 1915), p. 22.
[2]Martin Luther, *Die Martin Luthers Werke,* Kritische Gesamtausgabe (Weimar: H. Boklars Nachfolger), 2:244-45, related in Richard Warren, *12 Dynamic Bible Study Methods* (Wheaton, Ill.: Victor Books, 1978), p. 155.
[3]Eckman, *Literary Primacy of the Bible,* pp. 38-39.
[4]John Crowe Ransom, *God Without Thunder* (1930; reprint ed., Hamden, Conn.: Shoe String, 1965).
[5]T. S. Eliot, *Essays Ancient and Modern* (London: Faber and Faber), pp. 93ff.

Chapter Five: How to Read the New Testament

[1]Bruce M. Metzger, *The New Testament: Its Background, Growth, and Content* (Nashville: Abingdon Press, 1965), p. 8.

[2]*The New Oxford Annotated Bible,* ed. Herbert May and Bruce M. Metzger (New York: Oxford University Press, 1973), pp. 670-71.

[3]Stephen Neill, *Jesus Through Many Eyes* (Philadelphia: Fortress Press, 1976), p. 2.

[4]The gist of the following, with some additions of detail, is from St. Augustine's *Harmony of the Gospels,* Nicene and Post-Nicene Fathers, vol. 6, ed. Philip Schaff (Grand Rapids, Mich.: Eerdmans, 1979), pp. 80ff.

[5]Neill, *Jesus Through Many Eyes,* p. 119.

[6]Donald Guthrie, *New Testament Introduction* (Downers Grove, Ill.: InterVarsity Press, 1970), p. 336.

[7]Here I purposefully leave aside the opinion of the majority of New Testament scholars who believe that Paul was not actually the author of 1 and 2 Timothy and Titus. Questions are also frequently raised concerning Ephesians and Colossians. But although it is of little concern to us here, I will say that I feel arguments *for* the Pauline authorship of all of these letters are sufficiently impressive to use the usual designation without excessive quibbling.

[8]Ian Robinson, *The Survival of English* (Cambridge: At the University Press, 1973), p. 56.

Chapter Six: How to Read the Old Testament

[1]Pinchas Lapide and Jürgen Moltmann, *Jewish Monotheism and Christian Trinitarian Doctrine* (Philadelphia: Fortress Press, 1981), p. 27.

[2]Ibid., p. 30.

[3]Ransom, *God Without Thunder,* p. 45.

[4]Ibid.

[5]Abraham Joshua Heschel, *Man Is Not Alone* (New York: Harper, 1951), p. 129.

[6]Quoted in Ransom, *God Without Thunder,* p. 106.

[7]H. Wheeler Robinson, *Religious Ideas of the Old Testament* (London: Duckworth, 1956), p. 40.

[8]Ibid.

[9]Matthew Arnold, *Literature and Dogma* (New York: The Macmillan Company, 1914), pp. 23-24. Biblical and Apocryphal quotations are from Prov 12:28; 11:19; 8:15; 29:18; 3:17; Baruch 3:13; Deut 6:6-7; Prov 7:3; 3:3; 4:13.

Chapter Nine: Your Devotional Life: The Heart of Bible Study

[1]Frederic W. Farrar, *History of Interpretation,* reprint of 1885 Bampton lectures (Grand Rapids, Mich.: Baker, 1961), p. 328.

[2]Chrysostom *Homilies on St. Matthew* 64.3.

[3]Quoted in Eckman, *The Literary Primacy of the Bible,* p. 86.

[4]Herman Melville, *Moby Dick* (New York: Signet, 1980), pp. 21-22.

[5]Thomas à Kempis, *Of the Imitation of Christ* (Charlotte, N.C.: Commissions Press, 1963), pp. 46-47.

[6]Kurt Aland, *Four Reformers* (Minneapolis: Augsburg, 1979), p. 79.

[7]Edwin Hatch, "Breathe on Me, Breath of God," *Baptist Hymnal* (Nashville: Baptist Sunday School Board, 1956).

[8]Walter Trobisch, *Martin Luther's Quiet Time* (Downers Grove, Ill.: InterVarsity Press, 1975).

[9]George Buttrick, ed., *Interpreter's Bible*, 5 vols. (Nashville: Abingdon Press, 1962), 1:170.

[10]Ibid.

[11]Augustine *On Christian Doctrine* 2.41.

Chapter Ten: Bible Study in the Family

[1]Richard M. Weaver, *Ideas Have Consequences* (Chicago: University of Chicago Press, 1948), p. 148.

Chapter Eleven: Bible Study in the Church

[1]Melville, *Moby Dick*, p. 363.

[2]James Orr, *The Christian View of God and the World* (Grand Rapids, Mich.: Eerdmans, 1954), pp. 20-21, quoted in John R. W. Stott, *Your Mind Matters* (Downers Grove, Ill.: InterVarsity Press, 1972), p. 20.

[3]Quoted by Robinson, *The Survival of English*, p. 40.

[4]D. H. Lawrence, "John Galsworthy," *Phoenix* (1936), p. 545.

Chapter Twelve: Bible Study and World Missions

[1]"The Ballad of East and West" by Rudyard Kipling (1889).

[2]Arnold, *Literature and Dogma*, p. 73.